PRAISE FOR *A WARRIOR'S FAITH*

"Ryan Job was an inspiration to Chris Kyle. Ryan's death—and the death of Marc Lee—were two of the most important reasons Chris asked me to help him write *American Sniper*. Until I read *A Warrior's Faith* I really never understood the depth of that inspiration. Spiritual, compelling, and true to the SEAL's core belief: never quit. A must read!"

—SCOTT MCEWEN, COAUTHOR OF THE #1 *NEW YORK TIMES* BESTSELLER *AMERICAN SNIPER*, *EYES ON TARGET*, AND THE NATIONAL BEST-SELLING SNIPER ELITE SERIES, *ONE WAY TRIP* AND *TARGET AMERICA*

"I had the great honor to know Ryan Job as a SEAL brother and also as a member of the small unique fraternity within the brotherhood who have been shot in the head and survived. *A Warrior's Faith* captures the essence of Ryan Job—from his hysterical dry wit to his relentless 'overcome' mindset that I have built my own life around. Robert Vera did a great job telling Ryan's story of faith. It is a story that will motivate and inspire, have you laughing and crying, and more than anything, bring you to understand the caliber of a man in his walk of faith."

—JASON REDMAN, US NAVY SEAL (RETIRED) AND AUTHOR OF *THE TRIDENT: THE FORGING AND REFORGING OF A NAVY SEAL LEADER*

"Robert Vera really captures the intensity of the medical and combat situation in Ramadi in 2006. When reading his account, one feels that he or she is actually there in Charlie Medical with the doctors and medics who fought to save lives. I should know, because I was."

—ZACK KITCHEN, RETIRED MILITARY PHYSICIAN AND AUTHOR OF *THE UNBELIEVER*

A WARRIOR'S
FAITH

Navy SEAL Ryan Job, a Life-Changing Firefight, and the Belief That Transformed His Life

ROBERT W. VERA

NELSON
BOOKS

An Imprint of Thomas Nelson

Published in Nashville, Tennessee, by Nelson Books, an imprint of Thomas Nelson. Nelson Books and Thomas Nelson are registered trademarks of HarperCollins Christian Publishing, Inc.

Published in association with MacGregor Literary, Inc., PO Box 1316, Manzanita, OR 97130.

Interior designed by James A. Phinney.

Thomas Nelson titles may be purchased in bulk for educational, business, fundraising, or sales promotional use. For information, please e-mail SpecialMarkets@ThomasNelson.com.

The names and identifying characteristics of some individuals have been changed to protect their privacy.

Unless otherwise noted, Scripture quotations are taken from THE NEW KING JAMES VERSION. © 1982 by Thomas Nelson, Inc. Used by permission. All rights reserved.

Scripture quotations marked NIV are taken from the Holy Bible, New International Version', NIV'. Copyright © 1973, 1978, 1984, 2011 by Biblica, Inc.™ Used by permission of Zondervan. All rights reserved worldwide. www.zondervan.com

Scripture quotations marked KJV are from the KING JAMES VERSION.

Library of Congress Cataloging-in-Publication Data

Vera, Robert Jr., 1966-
  A warrior's faith : a decorated Navy SEAL, a brutal firefight, and the belief that transformed his life / Robert Vera Jr.
    pages cm
  Includes bibliographical references.
  ISBN 978-1-4002-0678-0
  1. Job, Ryan, 1981-2009. 2. United States. Navy. SEALs--Biography. 3. Iraq War, 2003-2011--Campaigns--Iraq--Ramadi. 4. Disabled veterans--United States--Biography. 5. Blind--Rehabilitation--United States--Biography. 6. Camp Patriot. 7. Christian biography. I. Title. II. Title: Decorated Navy SEAL, a brutal firefight, and the belief that transformed his life.
  V63.J57.V47 2015
  956.7044'345--dc23
  [B]

                          2014023949

Printed in the United States of America

15 16 17 18 19 RRD 6 5 4 3 2

To Haylee and Matthew

CONTENTS

CONTENTS

AUTHOR'S NOTE

THE EVENTS IN this book are true. The events related to Ryan Job's service in Ramadi, Iraq, have already been made public in part by various other sources including books, magazines, newspaper articles, and military award citations. I have constructed the dialogue from my journal writings, interviews, conversations, and memory. Thus, the dialogue may not be exactly word for word, but the meaning of what was said is accurate. For security reasons I have changed the names of many of the key people in this story.

Ryan Job was a Navy SEAL. He and I first met in early summer 2008. I am not, nor have I ever been, a Navy SEAL. Ryan and I crossed paths for a brief time, just long enough to change the course of both our lives forever. This is an amazing story of transformation, of how Ryan's life changed when he invested in his faith. Ryan's faith allowed him to literally climb mountains. His faith also helped transform many who knew him, including me. I write this book to share our story and introduce you to my friend Ryan Job, who was much greater than a highly decorated Navy SEAL and warrior.

—R.W.V.

FOREWORD

IT WAS A beautiful summer night in July on Mt. Rainier in Washington State, typical for that kind of year. You know, a million stars in the sky, fifteen degrees, thirty-mile-per-hour wind gusts, snow on the ground, and nowhere to go but up or down. Left or right was not an option unless we wanted to turn this mountain-climbing excursion into a free-fall experience. So we were going up. Typical, I guess, if you are a goat.

The frozen snow crunched beneath our feet as spikes pierced the glacier trying to grab some traction. Like a cruel, never-ending stair-master the mountain kept coming, and we kept climbing, adding one more step to the thousands we had already made. One more step, crunch, one more step, crunch. On and on, up and up we went.

I was smoked and falling off the pace. I could feel that I was the one holding up the team because the rope kept being pulled taunt by the guy in front of me, meaning he was moving faster than I was. The nylon rope we had tied to each other was life insurance in case the spikes didn't do their job and gravity took charge of the situation (which it always does when balancing on the side of an iced-over glacier). Fortunately for me, the team leader was merciful and wise. "Time to rest," he said. "Thank God," I whispered to myself.

I plopped down by a rock and stared out into the darkness. When you climb Rainier in July you must start out at night so that you get the bulk of the movement done before the sun comes up. Because come morning time, that big heat tab in the sky starts warming up the glacier, which is *no bueno*. When you are walking on the side of said glacier and it melts, you have a tendency to go where the melting ice travels, which is down the mountain very fast. Two mountaineering deaths occur each year on average on Rainier because of rock and ice fall, avalanches, and hypothermia associated with the severe weather.

I was breathing heavy, sucking wind hard, wondering who put the rocks in my ruck sack, because this mountain was kicking my butt.

"Man, they're going too fast," I complained to no one but myself. "We've got wounded warriors making this climb. We've got to slow down. I know I'm in shape. I can only imagine what they are going through."

I was starting to feel sorry for myself. The cold, the hurt, the effort was chipping away at my intestinal fortitude, and I started to snivel.

"My legs are on fire. I can't breathe. I don't really want to get to the top anyway. I can just volunteer to go back down with the stragglers and quietly bow out. No one will know."

The enemy within me was beginning to gain a strong hold, filling my mind with propaganda: I wasn't good enough; I was too weak; I didn't have what it takes. What was worse was that I was starting to believe it. I was ready to quit, and that would have been right about the time Ryan Job showed up.

"How you doing, Ranger?" Came a voice from the body next to me in the dark. That voice belonged to Ryan Job, a Navy SEAL who was one of the wounded warriors we were there to support through one of Camp Patriot's programs for wounded veterans. Camp Patriot is a God-centered nonprofit organization that provides outdoor adventure excursions for wounded and disabled veterans.

I tried to laugh it off and put up a good front.

"I'm good to go, my friend. It's just a mountain, can't beat me."

Ryan heard the truth in there somewhere and laughed back. "Yeah, false motivation is better than no motivation at all, huh?"

"No doubt. How are you doing?" I asked.

"Dude, I'm not gonna lie. I'm hurting," Ryan confessed.

"Me too," I admitted. "I can't feel my feet."

Like a comedian with spot-on timing—almost as if I'd been set up for it—Ryan hit me with a perfectly played shot: "Well, quit bragging, my feet are killing me too!"

With that Ryan pushed himself up, and it was time to roll.

As his guide came to lead him away, Ryan turned and left me with these words to think about for the rest of the climb to the top: "Come on, Ranger. You can do this"

He may as well have just said, "Come on, Mr. Big Shot Ranger. Don't you dare let a blind Navy SEAL beat you to the top."

You know, for a blind guy, Ryan sure had incredible vision. He saw right through my tough-guy camouflage. He knew I was smoked because he was too. But more importantly what Ryan saw was someone in need of encouragement, and he was going be that encouragement despite his own suffering.

This is the heart of servant leadership. It was engrained in him as a Navy SEAL. Take care of your buddy, because in the thick of the fight, all you have is each other. The only way you will make it back, by the grace of God, is if those guys to your left and right are there to cover you. So you do everything you can to ensure their success. You provide purpose, direction, and motivation. You stand up; drive on; say, "Follow me!"; and you lead the way, despite whatever pain you may be suffering.

Your body is pleading with you to quit, and your mind is telling you that you can't. But don't you believe them. You haven't checked in with your heart yet. Your heart will tell you something completely different. It will tell you the truth. Which is: "Yes, you can. You have everything you need. You have the intestinal fortitude required to drive on and complete the mission. You are qualified!"

The truth is you do have what it takes because you have God on your side, and he has given you strength. This is called character, and character is built upon the stormy billows of hardship, trials, tests, tragedies, and tribulations. This is a solid principle, and if it motivates you, then I would encourage you to read this book page by page.

Robert Vera, the author and one of Ryan Job's close friends, honors the life of one man who overcame and offers an inspiring illustration of a simple and biblical truth: If you believe, have faith, and stay strong, it's astounding what you can and will accomplish.

This is a story of faith and transformation. It is a story of how Ryan Job's faith influenced many others. We need more men like Ryan Job, and, instead, now we have less. I hope you find this story a light that will inspire, motivate, and remind you that you too have everything you need to be an example for others to follow. There is no limit to what you can accomplish when you surrounded yourself with people of strong character and have God on your side.

"Be strong and courageous. Do not be afraid; do not be discouraged, for the LORD your God will be with you wherever you go" (Joshua 1:9 NIV).

Keni Thomas

American country music singer and
former United States Army Ranger

PART ONE ★★★

TESTED

Chapter One

MY BOOK OF JOB

★ ★ ★

FOR THE RECORD, I don't believe in coincidences. There is a plan for each of us, a force that brings us together, then twists and binds us into a single length of rope attached to our shared destiny. You were meant to read these words. This story is for you and is now part of your plan.

The last sight Navy SEAL Ryan Job ever saw clearly was the glare of the sun on the battlefield, followed by a bright flash from a window of a faraway building. Less than a second later, a chain of events began that would alter the trajectory of his life. They would transform him physically, emotionally, and spiritually into a man whose story inspires everyone who knows it. It's a hard story to hear in some ways—a story of pain and loss and sacrifice. But it's also a story of hope and triumph.

There are amazing parallels between the life of Ryan Job and the Job in the Bible (both are pronounced *Jobe*). They were both good men who were tested and then transformed by the way they responded to their own suffering and loss. Suffering and loss are part of the human condition; we are all subject to them. How we react to our own suffering reveals our true character and individual greatness. Both the Job of the Bible and Ryan Job could have reacted to their experiences by living the rest of their lives as victims. However, both Ryan and the Job in the Bible chose a braver, better way, what some might call the hero's way.

Ryan acted greater than all the adversities in his life. This is what we admire about all our heroes: their uncommon acts in response to life's greatest challenges. Heroes run toward, not away from, burning buildings and the sounds of gunshots, cries, and sirens. Heroes put others ahead of themselves. Heroes work long hours to give their children better lives. Heroes pick us up when we are down and pull us from the wreckage of our own lives. Heroes act greater than the people around them. Heroes stand terrified on the cliff of danger and then step forward anyway. Ryan Job was a hero not just because of what he did *in* war but rather because of what he did *after* war.

The biblical story of Job is one of the oldest stories in Scripture. Job was a blameless and righteous man who had everything. God permitted Satan to test Job to prove Job's unyielding faith in God's grace and goodness. He allowed Satan to take away Job's vast wealth, his beloved family, and his health; yet through it all, Job stood steadfast in his faith and acted greater than his circumstances. Job trusted that his Redeemer was real. Through the process, Job was transformed by his suffering, and in the end Satan was rebuked and God restored all of Job's riches, and more. Rather than becoming a victim, Job turned into someone greater, an Old Testament hero whose example has given courage and hope to the world for thousands of years.

Ryan Job's story bears an uncanny resemblance to the life of his biblical namesake. He had every reason to become a victim, to retreat into bitterness. Instead, just like the Bible character, he took advantage of a life-altering event to survey what he believed and why. What he discovered inspired him to invest in his faith and make fundamental changes in how he lived. Instead of becoming a victim, he became a hero, though he never saw himself as one. The circumstances that he found himself in forced him to think differently about his life, and these new thoughts led to new beliefs. His new beliefs led to new behaviors, which led to a new lifestyle and, thus, a trans-formed life.

Many Bible scholars tell us that the book of Job is a ratio-nale for why bad things happen to good people. I have read the book of Job many times and can't find any evidence to support this theory. I believe that the lesson of Job is that pain, suffering, and faith all combine to become the neces-sary crucible that transforms a life from an ordinary one to an extraordinary one. Faith gives us the assurance that pain has a purpose in our lives—we just don't know what it is yet. What was unique about Job was not his intense suffering but rather his response to it. He accepted it with grace and humility, one time even thanking God for it.

Frederick Douglass, a former slave and brilliant thinker, explained suffering best when he wrote, "If there is no strug-gle there is no progress. Those who profess to favor freedom and yet depreciate agitation, are men who want crops without plowing up the ground, they want rain without thunder and lightning. They want the ocean without the awful roar of its many waters. This struggle may be a moral one, or it may be a physical one, and it may be both moral and physical, but it must be a struggle."[1] Ryan's story is proof that pain, loss, and suffering have a purpose in our lives and are part of a greater plan.

Ryan's story has been chronicled in a number of books and films, including the book *The Sheriff of Ramadi* by Dick Couch, the film *Act of Valor*, the book *Service: A Navy SEAL at War* by Marcus Luttrell, the bestselling memoir *American Sniper* by Chris Kyle, and the movie adaptation of *American Sniper* produced and directed by Clint Eastwood. Chris was one of Ryan's closest friends, and he dedicated his book to Ryan: "I'd also like to dedicate the book to the memory of my SEAL brothers Marc [Lee] and Ryan [Job], for their courageous service to our country and their undying friendship to me. I will bleed for their deaths the rest of my life."[2] I later came to know Chris through Ryan. Chris and Ryan served together on the battlefield with their Navy SEAL team the day Ryan's transformation began. After the war and by what some would call a coincidence, my life and both of theirs wove together for a brief time. The coincidences pile up to the point that you have to consider Einstein's observation that a coincidence is God's way of working anonymously.

Ryan was a tough Navy SEAL, a true warrior, and an American patriot. He was also a devoted husband, loving father, and a loyal friend. The way he and I met is inexplicable and unlikely. And though we only knew each other a short time, it was long enough to alter the course of my life forever. I write this story to honor Ryan and those he respected and loved, and as a way of saying thanks to him for showing me how to live fully— ruthlessly abandoning my old life in order to embrace a new one full of adventure, faith, and trust. *This* is my book of Job.

TOP GUN AMBITION

Ryan Job was the oldest of three children whose family had a long history of military service. His grandfather was a pilot in World War II. Ryan's lifelong dream was to be a Navy SEAL, a member of the elite Special Forces team that fought on sea, air, and land. Then after a few years, he'd trade his rifle for a joystick to fly jets as a Top Gun pilot. After his military career was over, he'd marry a beautiful woman with a great smile and live on a ranch with a horde of kids and pets. Together they would hunt and fish and live a life of adventure.

Ryan grew up in Issaquah, Washington, a suburb of Seattle. He loved history, science, and the outdoors. He was an above-average athlete with a strong work ethic and no ego, which made him a great leader. He spent most of his free time hunting and fishing.

When he was fourteen, Ryan latched on to his dream and started reeling it in. Since having a private pilot's license would improve his chances of being a Navy flyer, he saved nearly $20,000 for flying lessons by working after school as a janitor.

Within two years he had his license. Even as a teenager, Ryan had an extraordinary capacity for hard work, an unwavering faith, and a fierce determination when it came to achieving a goal he had set for himself.

Ryan was smart and determined but, by his own admission, not much interested in school. College was a box he needed to check off, but he wouldn't let it get in the way of his real desires. In 2002, after three years at the University of Washington, he dropped out to join the Navy at the age of twenty-two. He was living his dream.

GLADIATOR SCHOOL

Coincidentally, many years before I ever met or knew Ryan Job, I heard about his standout performance in SEAL training. Sean Carter, a good friend from my hometown of Boston, had joined the Navy with hopes of becoming a SEAL. The grueling SEAL training program is called Basic Underwater Demolition/SEAL, or BUD/S. The attrition rate is nearly 90 percent; a higher percentage of candidates make it into the NFL from the college football ranks than survive BUD/S. All Navy SEAL candidates are grouped into BUD/S classes and each class is assigned a specific number. Sean and Ryan started BUD/S in the same training class. Most of Sean's tales about his experiences included a guy named Jobie. He was the brunt of every instructor's abuse, but he took their torture with such a great attitude that they eventually came to love him for it.

Ryan and Sean arrived at the BUD/S training facility on

the same day and at the exact same time, unknown to each other when they walked through the gated entrance together. The two became fast friends, and soon Jobie's stories began filtering back to me even before "indoc," the indoctrination program to prepare raw recruits for the challenge of BUD/S. Instructors had the candidates line up for inspection and information. Ryan stood in his blue Navy uniform complete with traditional dog bowl hat. He was singled out immediately because of his build. Though he was strong, he was not the lithe, athletic type; he was heavy for his height. He referred to himself as "husky." One of the instructors saw what he thought was a weak link and ordered Ryan to demonstrate the O-course for all the others.

The O-course, or obstacle course, began with a progression of logs fashioned into hurdles that increased in height. Stronger than a bull and built like a bulldozer, Ryan got off to a good start. But when he jumped from the four-foot-high log to the six-foot-high log, he ended up hanging upside down.

My friend Sean described the scene:

All 250 of us stood there in silence watching him hang upside down. After about a minute, sweat started dripping from his forehead in a steady stream, but nobody said a word. Gravity, his sweaty hands, and his husky build were all conspiring against him. We all expected him to drop and were hoping somehow he'd land on his feet. But Ryan let out a primordial grunt and righted himself. Then, nimble as a cat, he danced to the finish of the O-course. It was like watching a bulldozer do the foxtrot. The instructors were silent—in shock, I suppose—until one of them walked up to him and said, "Job, today you have joined the ranks of the gladiators." Ryan offered a slight grin.

Ryan told me that if it were not for Sean, he may not have passed BUD/S, or at least not the timed run test. BUD/S consists of three phases. In order to make it past the first phase, all candidates are required to complete a four-mile run course in under thirty-two minutes while wearing combat boots. The run course is a soft sandy beach; running in sand is like running in mud. Running eight-minute miles for four miles in sand wearing boots is tough for even the most agile and fittest of athletes. "My passion for food made the run a little more challenging for me than the other candidates," Ryan admitted.

Running in sand requires a unique gliding or skimming-like stride that is altogether different from the normal "strike and push" running technique. Ryan especially hated running fast, and his technique was to finish any way possible. The instructors knew that Ryan would struggle on this test. Just before the run, one instructor walked up to Ryan and Sean, pointed at Ryan, and said, "If he fails, you both fail, and you're both gone." Ryan said that right from the start, Sean pushed him from behind as hard as he could and continued to do so the entire four miles. They both finished just under the thirty-two minute cut-off time. "There was this whining that sounded like over-stressed hydraulics; he was grunting, spitting, sputtering, coughing, and there were other awful sounds coming out of him. It was close, but we both made it," Sean recalled. Ryan was proud of his slow and steady, "deliberate" pace. He once told me that he had the speed of a narcoleptic sloth.

BUD/S was intense, and it became more so as instructors identified an individual's weaknesses and drilled down on them. "Most people despise being cold and wet," Ryan told me later. "The instructors knew this, so they would put us through surf torture every chance they got." Surf torture consisted of a group of trainees lying faceup in the shallow surf, arms locked together, as the sixty-degree Pacific water washed over them. A lot of people just up and quit in the first few days because they were too cold. But Ryan didn't mind surf torture, he explained to me, because he was like one of those dogs with a mass of fur that both keeps them warm and hides all the rippling muscle underneath. "My build naturally insulated me. I was always warm. Soon I noticed that people were jockeying for a position next to me during surf torture. That's the only time I was popular!"

The husky recruit was a marked man. The instructors—all hardened, ruthless Navy SEALs—mercilessly harassed him at every opportunity. His fellow classmates were sympathetic but happy that Ryan diverted the instructors' attention away from them. Ryan was rolled back from his original class more than once—meaning he had to drop back to repeat some training and join the class behind him—which made his stay in BUD/S significantly longer. "Ryan endured the worst possible 'legal' mental, physical, and emotional abuse from some of the hardest men on the planet, and he never even came close to cracking," offered a former BUD/S classmate. Near the end of the first phase of BUD/S, some of the hardest instructors became fond of the husky kid with the great attitude. Instead of the instructors breaking Ryan, he broke them, and they loved him!

As the class prepared for Hell Week, a Sunday/Saturday training evolution with little food or sleep, a BUD/S instructor was telling the class in a very loud voice that most of them would not make it. Most of them would quit and walk away. Then he walked directly over to Ryan and stood inches away from him, lowered his voice, and smiled. "Except for you, Job. Hell Week will be just like every other week around here for you." Ryan passed Hell Week with flying colors.

BUD/S was the crucible that tested and transformed Ryan physically. He would go on to finish all three phases of BUD/S, meeting every physical requirement and earning his Navy SEAL Trident. In the years to come he would be tested over and over and be transformed in other profound ways.

SEAL TEAM 3

Ryan said the abuse was a thousand times worse after he graduated from BUD/S and was assigned to his new SEAL team. "As a new guy, if your SEAL team does *not* harass you mercilessly, it means they don't like you," Ryan said. "Based on the consistency and severity of the abuse I took, there was no question that everyone on the team *really* liked me." Most new SEAL team guys suffer the generic frat-like initiations: drinking vile concoctions of booze and body fluids, shaving heads and eyebrows, and the like. "Unfortunately, I was assigned to a very creative and dedicated team; it seemed that they spent as much time planning my hazing as they did planning combat missions. It was like art to them, and after they finished with me, they would all sit back and admire their work."

The SEAL teammate who started out as one of Ryan's harshest critics eventually became one of his closest friends. Chris Kyle, a seasoned Navy SEAL, described Ryan's hazing in his bestselling book *American Sniper*:

> I think the new guy who made the biggest impression was Ryan Job. And the reason was that he did not look like a SEAL; on the contrary, Ryan looked like a big lump. Being a new guy we would have beat Ryan anyway, but his weight made things a lot worse for him. We actively tried to make him quit. But Ryan wasn't a quitter. You couldn't compare his determination to anyone else's. He was such a hard worker, so sincere, and so funny, that at some point we all just went, "I love you. You are the man." Because no matter how he looked, he truly was a SEAL. And a good one. We tested him, believe me.[3]

It's remarkable that Chris would choose the words, "We tested him." The same words were written about Job in the Bible: "But He knows the way that I take; when He has tested me, I shall come forth as gold" (Job 23:10). Ryan prevailed on every test.

For four years, Ryan took all the hazing and abuse aimed at him in stride, honed his skills, and bonded into the brotherhood of the SEAL teams. In April 2006, he arrived at his first combat duty station, 7,000 miles from home, in the most dangerous city in the world: Ramadi, Iraq.

Chapter Two

A MANY-SIDED STRUGGLE

★ ★ ★

HISTORY RINGS WITH the names of pivotal battles. These decisive moments are etched in our collective memory and need no explanation: the Alamo, Stalingrad, Waterloo, Gettysburg. In 2006, Ramadi joined the list. Gen. David Petraeus, the American commander in Iraq, compared the second Battle of Ramadi to the Battle of Stalingrad during World War II, possibly the bloodiest battle in human history, in which the Soviet Union and German forces were deadlocked in a stalemate battle for access to the Volga River.

Ramadi is a city of four hundred thousand people scattered along 25 miles of the Euphrates River in al-Anbar Province of central Iraq, 65 miles east of Baghdad. The desert stretches in every direction as far as the eye can see. Temperatures routinely reach 120 degrees. The city is a dusty collection of low-rise buildings, many of them bombed out and abandoned after years of war. Over the years, a mix of opposing religious and tribal factions grew relentlessly more contentious. By the summer of 2006, al-Anbar Province was one of the deadliest places on the planet: of the 4,802 US service members killed in the Iraq War, 1,335 died fighting in al-Anbar. Per capita, the provincial capital Ramadi was the deadliest city on earth.

GOING TO HELL

The enemy enjoyed many advantages in Ramadi. They could hide easily among the residents of the crowded city. Though the majority of Iraqis are Shia Muslims, Ramadi was almost entirely Sunni, the Shia's historic adversaries. Thus, Sunni foreign fighters who reached Ramadi could join fellow Sunnis in the fight against America and her allies. They could support the insurgency in the city or resupply on their way to other Sunni-controlled areas throughout the Sunni Triangle.

By the time Ryan Job reported for duty in Ramadi, the Sunni insurgency had been under way for years. In 2004, the commander of the Marine garrison in al-Anbar, Maj. Gen. James Mattis, had warned, "If we don't hold the providential capital [Ramadi], the rest of the province goes to hell."[1] It's likely that if the insurgents had succeeded in Ramadi, then all of Iraq and perhaps the entire region would have quickly spiraled out of control under the weight of a violent, many-sided power struggle.

On August 17, 2006, four months after Ryan arrived in Ramadi, Marine Chief of Intelligence Col. Pete Devlin issued a classified report entitled "State of the Insurgency in al-Anbar." The report began, "Al-Anbar has been lost and there was almost nothing that could be done. . . . We are no longer capable of defeating the insurgency in al-Anbar."[2] Not only were military operations at a stalemate, unable to extend and sustain security beyond the perimeters of their bases, but also regional governments in the province had collapsed, and the weak central government had almost no presence.

The Shia-Sunni civil conflict woven into the war made the task force's assignment nearly impossible. Ramadi is home to the largest group of Iraqi Sunnis. The Sunnis are the family tribe of long-time dictator Saddam Hussein, whom the American forces deposed. Although the tribe made up only 30 percent of Iraq's overall population, they enjoyed many privileges under Saddam. Thus, when the Americans removed Saddam, they also took away the Sunnis' privileged status in Iraq. Needless to say, because of that the Sunnis were hostile toward Americans.

The Shia Muslims made up about 60 percent of Iraq's population. The two Muslim denominations split after the death of Muhammad in AD 632 and have been in a "disagreement" ever since. The conflict is not just a friendly Yankees versus Red Sox rivalry—it is an abhorrence of each other's existence that has been passed down from one generation to another.

The Americans were working in Ramadi with the new Iraqi security force. These forces were made up mainly of Shia who were antagonistic toward the majority Sunni population in Ramadi. The forces included interpreters and soldiers assigned to work directly with American military personnel. The Sunni population resented the fact that Shia from other areas of Iraq were "invading" Ramadi with the Americans. The Sunnis viewed the Shia as hostile foreigners and treasonous spies.

Not helping matters was the fact that Shia gangs in other parts of the country had unleashed a special brand of pent-up aggression against their rival Sunnis, the kind of retribution that had simmered for twenty-four years under Saddam Hussein. These gangs carried out their violence on the Sunni population with impunity under the blind eye of the new Iraqi government security forces. Keep in mind that in order to end the conflict in Ramadi, the young American warriors needed to find a way to create an alliance between themselves and the Sunni tribe. They needed to accomplish this despite the removal of the Sunnis' revered leader, Saddam, and the 1,370-year deadly rift between Sunnis and Shias, and they had to do it while being shot at. This was the Ramadi, Iraq, that Ryan and his SEAL team were sent to liberate.

COLLATERAL DAMAGE

On Ryan's very first mission in Iraq, he and his team got into a gunfight. Eighty percent of his missions involved gunfights with the enemy. He quickly experienced the personal aspect of war: at its most basic, war is one person desperately working to kill another. We apply euphemisms to try to lessen the humanity of the conflict. But a "casualty" is someone's son or daughter killed, wounded, or missing in battle. There's nothing casual about it. "Collateral damage" refers to civilian husbands, wives, fathers, mothers, children, and grandparents in the wrong place at the wrong time. Each of them had friends they laughed with, memories they cherished. They had favorite foods and dreams of the future.

Television news displays a version of war that viewers want to see, sanitized and impersonal. The truth is too damaging, too raw, too ruthless. The truth would keep America awake with nightmares. We're outraged at a school shooting where dozens of innocent children are killed. In war, this happens every day. But there's no outrage because "it's war," and the war dead aren't teachers and children, they're just "collateral damage."

Ryan saw the collateral damage close up. On one mission, Ryan and one of his SEAL team's medics, Tommy, worked to save the life of an older Iraqi man who had just been shot. Ryan was fairly certain the guy was an enemy insurgent. The enemy blended seamlessly into the population, and they used it for cover as they probed, planted bombs, and took random shots at American troops. Ryan described the incident:

He was older, looked to be in his sixties, and the wheelbarrow he was pushing seemed heavy and was covered with a tarp. It was impossible to tell if he was transporting a bomb, rocks, or something else. He entered what was clearly a restricted area, and soon after a shot rang out. He was hit and squirming on the ground from a sucking chest wound; I had never seen that type of wound before. I was helping Tommy, who was frantically working to save the guy. As he was treating him, the man's face became twisted and distorted; he looked like an alien as he gasped for breath. Then, all of a sudden, he just died.

Another time there was a young Iraqi soldier—*jundi* in Arabic—whom Ryan was helping to train along with several others. Ryan's SEAL team had taken the group to secure a building suspected of housing terrorists. Ryan was prone on the ground, manning his bipod machine gun, when he saw some of the trainees moving into a potential field of fire. Ryan asked the jundi to man his machine gun while he crossed the street to move the trainees out of the area.

Suddenly a violent burst of AK-47 fire rang out toward his previous position. Ryan ran back to find the young soldier dead. An insurgent had moved to a window position and fired down on the man as he manned Ryan's machine gun. "His head was basically gone," Ryan explained. The young Iraqi was about Ryan's age and had a family.

It could easily have been Ryan who was shot that day. Was it luck that he had walked across the road? Another coincidence? Or an invisible hedge of protection that had saved his life?

Ryan Job deployed to Ramadi in April 2006 as a member of SEAL Team 3, Task Unit Bruiser, Charlie Platoon. His team's mission was to join together with airmen, Marines, and soldiers of the First Armored Division to defeat a well-established insurgency in the city. Their strategy was to "seize, clear, hold, and build." Once the city was secured, they were to turn it over to the Iraqi national government.

This seemingly clear and straightforward strategy was complicated by the mix of enemy combatants: Sunni Muslim militias, Mujahedeen insurgents, Iranian trained snipers, the international Islamic terrorist faction Al-Qaeda in Iraq, and organized criminals exploiting the region for profit. Ryan put it in simple terms: "Basically, there were lots of different groups of people trying to kill us." The Americans' success depended on persuading the Sunni Muslims to switch sides and join them in defeating Al-Qaeda in Iraq, which was also made up exclusively of Sunni Muslims. Of all the factions, Al-Qaeda in Iraq was the most dangerous because of its use of suicide bombings and kidnappings.

Al-Anbar Province is home to the Sunni Triangle, 100 miles on each side with points at Ramadi on the west, Baghdad on the east, and Saddam Hussein's hometown of Tikrit on the north. The triangle's capital of brutality was Ramadi, the Iraqi headquarters of Al-Qaeda in Iraq and its leader, Abu Musab al-Zarqawi (who was seen beheading hostages in a series of infamous YouTube videos). Money, weapons, and fighters freely flowed into the city from Jordan, Syria, and Saudi Arabia. Insurgents who had abandoned their positions in Baghdad and Fallujah, a city a few miles away along the Euphrates River, had consolidated their resources and firepower in Ramadi. It was the enemies' new front.

Men like Ryan Job were there to make sure that the city did not fall under the complete control of Al-Qaeda in Iraq. The American task force was fighting a massive Sunni tribal army that had an endless supply of new fighters, many of whom were state sponsored with weapons, training, and money. In the summer of 2006, the Second Battle of Ramadi was in full swing, and the city was a tangled web of hatred and death.

THE ALLEY

Shortly after arriving in Ramadi in 2006, Ryan was serving as his platoon's automatic weapons gunner as he and his SEAL team moved through one of the city's countless narrow alleys. All of a sudden bullets started flying at them from all directions. The team was pinned down, sprayed with automatic weapon fire and everything else the insurgents could throw at them. "There was little cover," Ryan told me, "and everyone was piled up in back of a narrow wall when the enemy began directing all their fire at us. I knew that if I didn't do something, we would all be killed. The team initiated an immediate action maneuver by returning fire and performing a column peel. Totally exposed to the enemy fire with no cover, I engaged the insurgents with my machine gun." Ryan stepped into the center of the alley and laid down furious cover fire, allowing his SEAL team a brief moment to evacuate the alley. Ryan continued:

> I could see the bullets coming at me in slow motion. They hit everything around me—trash piles, water puddles—dozens of rounds coming at me and not one touched me. It was like I had a force field around me. I remember looking through my sunglasses and seeing bright flashes directly in front of me, a strange occurrence because muzzle flashes are not normally visible in daylight. I remember watching pieces of garbage and puddle water kicking up just feet from my knee as bullets ricocheted all around. I distinctly recall seeing bullet holes riddle up a wall next to my head.

With my platoon peeling behind me, I fired every round in my pouch, praying that my rounds would hit the incoming fire in midair before it struck me.

Nearly everyone on the team was shot except Ryan. "After the ambush," Ryan said, "one of our guys couldn't figure out why his CamelBak was drained of water. He filled it up before we went out and hardly drank any. After a closer inspection he found a bullet hole in the bottom of it that emptied all his water out." Once again, a hedge of protection seemed to surround Ryan, affording him safety and protection beyond explanation.

I had known Ryan for a year before he told me that story, and he only told me because, in a shoebox in his closet, we found the Bronze Star he'd been awarded for his heroic action that day. There were other medals too.

When I asked him if he was scared, he said, "I wasn't really scared or amped up at that moment; I was just focused on the task at hand. And if anything, I was more afraid of letting my teammates down than I was of being shot."

That was Ryan. Some have described him as "fearless," but I knew better. Ryan was afraid, but he acted anyway. Action in the face of fear is what courage is all about. He acted because he loved his SEAL brothers. They trained, fought, bled, and sacrificed together. In that alley, Ryan's fear of injury or death was cast away by the greater fear that one of his friends would be wounded or killed if he didn't take action.

Ryan taught me that in war, when the fighting starts, no

man is thinking about—or willing to die for—his country. Warriors risk their lives to save each other. And they would have it no other way. Ryan Job was this type of warrior.

COVER FIRE

Ryan held true to his principles even when it meant disobeying authority. On one particular mission, he was out with Chris Kyle and a group of other SEALs, Marines, and Iraqi jundis providing cover for a unit of advancing Marines. Ryan's crew had occupied a tall building with a good view and were in position, scouting for the enemy. Not long after they set up, about a hundred enemy fighters started moving toward them. When Ryan and his group opened fire, insurgents focused all their weapons on the building where they were hiding. Incoming fire was so bad that they had to pull out and head back to a Marine outpost several hundred yards to the rear.

The crew split in half. Ryan's half evacuated the building while the other half, including Chris, covered their exit. By the time the first half of the group was safely back at the outpost, the remaining men were nearly surrounded and heavily outgunned. Chris wrote about that day:

> Ryan realized our predicament as soon as he arrived at the Marine outpost. He and the chief got into an argument over whether to provide cover for us. The chief claimed that their job was to stay with the Iraqi jundis, who were already hunkered down inside the Marine camp. The chief ordered

him to stay; Ryan told him what he could do with his order. Ryan ran upstairs on the roof of the Marine building, where he joined the Marines trying to lay down support fire for us, and we fought off the insurgents.[3]

Ryan's own words as he relayed the story to me were respectful of the Navy chief in question. Maybe the chief didn't know that Ryan's younger brother was a decorated Marine who had been involved in heavy fighting during his tours in Fallujah. Ryan and his brother were very close, and because of this Ryan felt a solemn responsibility to aid and support the Marines as well as his fellow SEALs, regardless of the consequences. Ryan always put others' needs and welfare before his own despite the risk. Ryan explained the episode:

> The chief had a number of good reasons why we should not go on the roof. I didn't see it as an option; we needed to get up on the roof to provide cover fire. Our guys were still out there, and going up to the roof to provide them cover was one of the least risky options for everyone involved, except the enemy. Besides, we're SEALs, the Spartan warriors of the American armed forces. We don't ask how many are the enemy, we simply ask: Where are they? I was not the only one on the roof. There were Marines up there with me. Our guys eventually made it back to the base safely.

Ryan was a new guy with only a few weeks of combat experience; conversely, the Navy chief was a senior leader with years of combat experience. Ryan played the incident down: "Rank in the SEAL teams is not what it is elsewhere in the Navy or other parts of the military. It was not like I was disobeying a direct order; he had his opinion and I had mine. It was really no big deal." Reading between the lines, I believe that the chief in question may have felt personally responsible for Ryan's safety and wanted to make sure that nothing happened to him.

Colonel Devlin's classified report made clear that Ramadi was all but lost. The insurgency, led by Sunni Al-Qaeda in Iraq, was in control. The only way to retake Ramadi was to defeat Al-Qaeda in Iraq. The best way to do that was to somehow win over the Sunni tribe. Ryan once asked me, "Do you know how to win a war?" Before I could answer, he replied, "Break the enemy's will to fight."

The last-ditch effort to retake the province was assigned to the joint military task force that included SEAL Team 3 and Ryan Job.

Chapter Three
"I'M OKAY"

★ ★ ★

EARLY ON THE morning of August 2, 2006, Ryan and Chris Kyle were on a rooftop of a four-story apartment building in Ramadi. The two men had entered the building together, and Ryan had cracked jokes as they walked up the stairwell to the roof. Their assignment was to cover the other members of their SEAL team on the ground below as they moved to clear the buildings and homes of enemy fighters. Chris was already in line for a Silver Star, the military's third-highest honor awarded for gallantry, for his actions in Ramadi.

Ryan and Chris were to provide protection from a city full of enemies, all of whom were desperate to kill them and their fellow SEALs. Ryan was situated slightly southeast, watching a vacant road as the morning sun pointed toward him. Chris was positioned diagonally from Ryan, facing west. He peered through the scope of his sniper rifle, searching for enemy targets that might attempt to do harm to his SEAL brothers. It was a slightly hazy, 98-degree morning in Ramadi with 24-percent humidity and a gentle northwest wind blowing straight at Ryan. The visibility was 5.6 miles, and the barometric pressure was on the rise. Snipers find these nearly perfect conditions for shooting.

Chris was a skilled sniper; he had already racked up more than ninety confirmed enemy kills, making him one of the most deadly marksmen in US military history. He was so accurate that insurgents put a $20,000 bounty on his head and dubbed him "The Devil of Ramadi." Snipers are professional shooters, and they have been known to change the course of a battle. This happened during the Civil War Battle of Spotsylvania Court House, when Sergeant Grace of the Confederate Army sniped and killed Maj. Gen. John Sedgwick at the incredible distance of 800 yards. The death of Sedgwick delayed the Union's attack, leading to a Confederate victory.

Ryan knelt on the warm roof, hunched over his machine gun with his chin tucked tight into his gunstock. His clear-blue eyes were covered by dark sunglasses that dimmed the glare of the morning sun, the safety of his weapon was clicked off, and his right index finger was hooked lightly around the trigger. There was an eerie stillness to the city that morning, a quiet that penetrated everywhere and flushed out familiar sounds. Ryan could hear footsteps rising up from the streets below. He could hear the rhythm of his heart pounding in his ears and his breath exiting his body; this rhythm calmed and focused him as he gazed down at the street. As Ryan and Chris scanned for targets, another shooter was scanning for them. Hidden by the glare of the rising sun, an enemy marksman centered a human head in the crosshairs of his rifle scope. The shooter's heart rate and breathing, the air temperature, and the target distance all blended and pulsed together as he centered the crosshairs on his enemy's head and squeezed the trigger.

A single gunshot broke the morning silence. It was sharp and deliberate, and its echo slid over buildings and streets and rolled directly toward Ryan and Chris. Instinctively, the SEAL team working the streets below took cover. Chris fell to the floor and lay motionless for a moment, then checked himself for holes and blood; he was unharmed. He then called to his fellow SEALs to make sure none of them were hurt. His teammates answered back and were all accounted for. Last he called to Ryan, who lay slack and still over his weapon. "Ryan! *Ryan!*" Ryan didn't respond. Chris called out again, "Ryan, quit screwing around!" But Ryan lay motionless, slumped over his weapon, resting on his right arm like he was taking a nap in the middle of the war. Chris sensed there was something very wrong and made a desperate dash across the roof to Ryan. Chris rolled Ryan onto his side to find one half of Ryan's face gone. Fragments of a sniper's bullet had torn open his face. Ryan Job was twenty-five years old.

THE SHOOTER

A 7.62 × 54-millimeter bullet, about the size of a AA battery, had exited the enemy's sniper rifle at 1,400 mph. By the time it reached Ryan, atmospheric friction had heated it to more than 500 degrees Fahrenheit. The heat from a sniper's bullet has been known to cauterize wounds as it passes through the body. If the bullet had cleanly hit its target, Ryan Job would have been killed instantly. But the shot was low, striking Ryan's machine gun first, punching through his gun sight, and piercing his sunglasses before ripping through his right eye. Along the way the shrapnel shattered his sunglasses, adding shards of the lenses to the other deadly missiles. Within a heartbeat, the entire right side of his face was one massive open wound. His cheekbone and eye socket were blown away. His right eye was gone.

The shooter probably used a Russian Dragunov sniper rifle, highly prized by insurgents, who acquired them and their sniper training from Iran. The Dragunov can kill at 1,300 meters. Al-Qaeda in Iraq had a nasty habit of kidnapping pregnant woman and making them transport the rifles and other weapons across the city. After a few shipments— or sooner, if they felt the "mules" were being observed—the women were murdered.

Ryan's shooter was never identified. He could have been a local recruit or a foreign fighter trained and armed in Iran or Afghanistan. Iran's involvement in the Iraq war was an open secret. Among the trainers was Ali Mussa Daqduq, a seasoned twenty-four-year veteran of Lebanese Hezbollah, which was established and supported by Iran. Mr. Daqduq traveled from Iran to Iraq in the summer of 2006 to train groups of enemy snipers. He was later arrested in Iraq and turned over to the Iraqi government, who released him. Wherever Ryan's assailant came from, he likely was trained to shoot Americans in a specific order: snipers, officers, Special Forces soldiers, communications personnel, and then machine gunners. Ryan's Special Forces uniform and machine gun made him a high-value target.

MAN DOWN

Ryan was unconscious as a mixture of blood and bone fragments pooled in his throat. The rooftop was quickly soaked with his blood. Even at that early hour, the August sun had heated the roof to more than 100 degrees. The blood draining from Ryan's body simmered on the hot surface, filling the air with the scent of carnage. The odor is unmistakable: the smell that emergency responders, surgeons, and butchers can all intuitively identify.

Chris was well aware of the sniper strategy of shooting one man, waiting until help came, and then shooting the responders one at a time. Snipers call this "piling them up." Despite knowing he could be the unseen sniper's next target, Chris stayed by Ryan's side. Alone with Ryan on the rooftop, Chris felt sure that Ryan was going to die, and that the same enemy who had just shot Ryan was now bringing him into focus on his rangefinder grid. Ryan lay on the roof convulsing. Knowing an invisible enemy is about to strike can paralyze even the most seasoned warrior, but somehow Chris remained lucid and professional.

Years later, Chris and I talked about that day. He knew every second could mean the difference between life and death for Ryan. He was well aware of the "golden hour," the first sixty minutes after a major traumatic injury when medical treatment has the greatest lifesaving success rate. I asked Chris if he was hesitant about helping Ryan for fear of being shot. Chris replied:

It's a strange thing. Unless you have survived a sniper attack, you really don't know what's happening. Your brain does not work fast enough to connect the sound of a random gunshot to the sight of your friend lying on the ground to a sniper who may already have you in his crosshairs. I knew the situation immediately, and I was sure that I was going to get shot, but I needed to get to Ryan. I would have been useless if I stayed on the other side of that roof and got myself shot. I decided that if I was going to die, it would be helping Ryan. There were no two ways about it.

Chris Kyle was one of the world's foremost experts on weapons and field of fire. He instinctively decoded the shot's report and narrowed down the list of likely weapons and their range. With that he could approximate the sniper's location and move Ryan to a slice of the roof that would give them the most protection. Then Chris made an urgent radio call to the rest of the team on the street below. Usually his Texas accent gave a slow, calm, even tempo to his speech. Not at that moment. Loud, fast, and sharp, Chris roared into his radio, "Man down! Man down!"

THE HEDGE OF PROTECTION

Within minutes, the members of Ryan's SEAL platoon joined Chris on the roof. Defying the sniper, the team surrounded Ryan and worked together to save his life. Ryan's SEAL brothers were now his first responders. For them, the mission had changed. It was no longer to capture or kill the enemy—they were on a rescue mission for one of their own. Their assignment was to stop the bleeding, stabilize, and evacuate. Just as in the Civil War battle, the sniper had indeed changed the course of this fight.

Before the crack of the sniper's bullet split the morning air, the scene had been quiet. Now it seemed that this shot was the signal for the battle to begin. Bullets came from all directions, targeting the SEALs on the roof and on the ground. Ryan's rescuers were unfazed, exposing themselves to direct enemy fire as they worked to save their friend. In spite of the chaos all around them, they were calm, deliberate, and professional.

Chris later told me that Marc Lee, one of Ryan's closest friends, stood in the exact spot where Ryan was shot and provided cover fire, placing a barrage of bullets downrange at anything that resembled a threat. Chris stood opposite of Marc, scanning for targets. The sniper was still out there, likely watching and waiting for a clear shot at one of them. Tommy, one of the team's two medics, ran up to the roof and went to work to stop Ryan's bleeding.

Treating a head wound is different from treating other wounds. Applying too much pressure can cut off blood supply to a swollen brain and cause permanent brain damage or death. Ryan's SEAL commander, Luke, knew the seriousness of the wound from the bright-red color of the blood. It was from an artery, one of the vital pathways that supply the body's organs with freshly oxygenated blood directly from the lungs. A damaged artery deprives the body of oxygen. If it isn't quickly clamped off, the rupture becomes a death sentence.

Luke was Ryan's role model, the type of leader Ryan aspired to become: brilliant, strong, bold, highly effective, and confident, yet humble. Luke held Ryan's hand, calling to him, "Come on, Ryan, you're going to be okay, brother!" Luke was literally calling Ryan back into this world. "We're going to get you out of here! Come on!" Luke was calm and flawless in his work. He was later awarded the Silver Star for coordinating Ryan's rescue off the roof. Luke was actually wounded that same day pursuing the enemy who shot Ryan.

A study on Iraq War casualties found that severe head wounds had a mortality rate of 30 to 50 percent.[1] Head wounds are rated on the Glasgow Coma Scale, a neurological scale that aims to give a reliable, objective way of measuring the conscious state of a person. A patient is assessed against the criteria of the scale and given points. The points are then added up to generate a score between 3 and 15. The lowest possible score is a 3, which means deep coma or death, while the highest is 15, a fully awake person.[2] As Ryan lay motionless on the roof, he was a 3.

Tommy struggled to control the bleeding, and Luke kept talking to Ryan, hoping to bring him back to consciousness. Then Ryan Job, gravely wounded, half his face missing, suddenly sat up, coughed, and said, "I'm okay." He'd heard Luke's voice through the daze of semiconsciousness and knew his brothers were risking their lives to save him. The impact of the shot, he said later, felt like being hit in the face with a spike-shaped sledgehammer. But somehow he knew that the sooner he was out of there, the sooner his brothers would be out of danger. As Ryan struggled to his feet, Luke was still holding his hand in amazement. Tommy had to say, "Sir, please let go!" They all needed to get off that roof.

Luke helped Ryan to his feet and carried him a few yards to a safe area. Chris then picked up Ryan and slung him over his shoulder to carry him down off the roof. Ryan said to Chris, "Put me down. I'm good, I can walk." He refused to allow the enemy to make him a victim; he would not be a burden to his team. He could still see out of his left eye, and he said that he was "good to go." He knew his team needed every gun in the fight if they were to get out safely. "Marc had to shoot for me, and I didn't want to burden anyone else by having them carry me." And so, after losing half his face and a quarter of the blood in his body, Ryan evacuated himself from the roof while his fellow SEALs laid down cover fire.

Medivac to the hospital would not be easy. The battle raged all around, making helicopter extract impossible. The fact was that Ramadi was far too dangerous for helicopters to operate in the daylight. Fortunately, the US Army was working nearby with their Bradley armored fighting vehicles, which are built like small tanks. They rushed directly into the fight to evacuate Ryan. As Ryan was being evacuated in the Bradley, American tanks sprinted in to suppress the enemy fire.

Before I met Ryan, I had never known anyone outside the Bible named Job. When he described the scene as his SEAL brothers surrounded him under fire, protecting him and desperately trying to save his life, I was reminded of a passage in the Old Testament Book of Job that states God has always favored Job and has placed a hedge of protection around him (Job 1:10). The parallel is amazing. It wasn't the first time a hedge of protection had favored Ryan Job, and it wouldn't be the last.

MEDICAL SHACK

Tommy accompanied Ryan on a tense ride to the nearest medical outpost, a dilapidated building with no roof. The exposed nerves in Ryan's face caused excruciating pain as the Bradley jolted along the rutted road. Loss of blood had made him dizzy. He sat upright, leaning forward on his arm with a loose bandage around his head. Tommy remembered that he and Ryan had a normal conversation in the Bradley: "He must have been in incredible pain, but he was fully lucid."

At the medical aid station, an Army doctor was triaging the wounded. Ryan described what happened next. "Per standard operating procedure, and over Tommy's very adamant objection, the doctor wanted to place a breathing tube up my nose." While Tommy walked outside to clear his sidearm of bullets—another standard procedure in US medical aid stations that also treated enemy wounded—the attending doctor tried to insert a tube anyway. Tommy reentered the room just in time to see Ryan vomit about a gallon of blood over the terrified doctor.

Tommy rushed to Ryan and hovered over him. "This is my patient," he glared. "Don't touch him. We're leaving."

The medical staff in the shack had risked their own lives by moving close to the fighting in the hopes of saving lives. The staff was following protocol. However, the procedure the triage doctor was attempting could have pushed bone fragments into Ryan's brain and killed him.

Tommy knew what he was talking about. He and Ryan met at BUD/S, and after completing BUD/S, Tommy spent six months in an intensive training course to become a Special Forces medic. Equal to three years of specialized medical training, the intensive course known as 18 Delta prepares Special Forces medics to be de facto doctors on the battlefield. They're trained to do minor surgery, prescribe drugs, and deliver lifesaving trauma care. Among the many clinical rotations they're required to complete are emergency medicine, surgery, radiology, pediatrics, and obstetrics/gynecology. They also learn veterinary care because livestock is an important currency where Special Forces operate. One intense experience is the "goat lab," where a live goat is shot during a simulated firefight. To complete the course, candidates must save the goat.

Tommy wrapped a hedge of protection around Ryan as the two clambered back into the Bradley for a ride to the main hospital at Camp Ramadi.

CHARLIE MEDICAL

By coincidence, Camp Ramadi's hospital was home to Charlie Medical, a joint Army-Navy hospital that operated one of the busiest and best trauma centers in Iraq. The hospital was basically several dilapidated buildings with walls reinforced by plywood and sandbags. Ramadi offered few secure areas. Firefights, IEDs, and enemy rocket attacks could spring up anywhere in the city. The hospital at Camp Ramadi was no exception and was often the target of insurgent mortar attacks. Insurgents would "walk in" their bombs by aiming at a water tower directly behind the hospital. "The mortars would land very close. One hit a few feet from me and didn't detonate," said Lt. Cdr. John Homer, M.D., a former Navy Top Gun pilot who traded his wings for medical school and was the unit's anesthesiologist.

In general, the military is reluctant to place its medical personnel at risk in areas that are under nearly constant deadly attack, but it made an exception for the staff of Charlie Medical. Two highly skilled Navy surgeons and six medical technicians all volunteered for the Ramadi assignment. They provided around-the-clock surgical care to the severely wounded before transporting them to higher-level health care. "Nothing you read about in any medical or surgical textbook can prepare you for this type of environment," said Dr. Homer. Charlie Medical had a 98 percent success rate for stabilizing patients before sending them elsewhere for further treatment if necessary.

When they arrived at Charlie Medical, Tommy helped Ryan walk off the back of the Bradley; Ryan refused a stretcher and walked under his own power into the hospital. The trauma team was waiting for Ryan and swarmed him in a highly choreographed, well-practiced ballet that swept him directly into the operating room. Tommy stood aside and watched, helpless as his friend's fate was now in the hands of strangers.

"I remember him—his right cheek was open wide from his lip to his forehead. He sat upright on the examining table as we cut away his gear and worked on him," said Dr. Homer. "I've had a lot worse pain," Ryan said to the medical team as they worked to stop the bleeding and pump fluids back into his body. Dr. Homer recalled, "He was tough. He basically wanted us to sew him up so he could get back to the fight with his platoon. He had no idea how bad his wound was." Less than an hour after being severely wounded, Ryan underwent lifesaving surgery to stop him from bleeding out. If that surgical center had not been located at Camp Ramadi, Ryan would have been transported to another medical facility in Baghdad or Balad. If that had been the case, Ryan would have likely joined the other 30 to 50 percent of head wound victims who died from blood loss or other wound complications.

News that Ryan had been wounded spread fast through the task unit and the SEAL community. Chris, Tommy, and Ryan's other Navy SEAL teammates thought for sure that Ryan would never survive his wound; they all believed he was dead. Ryan was the first SEAL to be severely wounded in Iraq. This gave his SEAL team a renewed sense of urgency and commitment. Along with the rest of the task force, they continued to fight, moving fast and effectively, crushing the enemy and taking back areas of the city each day. They made history by changing the momentum of the war. Inch by inch, building by building, and finally street by street, they reclaimed Ramadi from the insurgents.

THE AWAKENING

After months of fighting, the impossible happened: the young warriors of the task unit convinced the Sunni tribes in Ramadi and all over Iraq to join with American forces against Al-Qaeda in Iraq. America's enemy became an ally in a phenomenon known as the Sunni Awakening. Some tribes of the Middle East don't recognize national laws or rules. They recognize only strength delivered and defended with ruthless force. While there is much speculation as to the various events leading up to the Awakening, my own extensive research leads me to believe that the Sunnis saw the momentum of the war change. Before running out of options, they allied themselves with the strongest partner, the Americans. Seeing Al-Qaeda in Iraq being destroyed every day at the hands of the task unit, they got a taste of a war they didn't want to lose. They tested the winds of war and partnered with the Americans, forming the Sons of Iraq to guard homes, streets, and critical infrastructure against gangs of thugs and Al-Qaeda in Iraq insurgents.

A year later, the United States began "the surge," flooding more than a hundred thousand new troops into Iraq, consolidating and extending the previous gains made by SEAL Team 3, the US Army First Brigade, and the rest of Task Unit Bruiser.

PART TWO ★★★

TRANSFORMED

Chapter Four

A PLACE OF HEALING

★ ★ ★

RYAN WAS TRANSFERRED from hospitals in Iraq to a military hospital in Germany, then back to the United States. He awoke from a medically induced coma at Bethesda Naval Medical Center to devastating news. The sniper's bullet had taken out his right eye, but as he walked off the rooftop under his own power after being wounded, he could still see out of his uninjured left eye. Now doctors broke the news that swelling in his head had cut off the flow of blood to the optic nerve of his left eye. The swelling interrupted the signal that is transmitted via a complex and fragile nerve network from the eye to the visual cortex in the back of the brain. The visual cortex is where the information transmitted by nerves is translated into images. Once damaged, the optic nerve never regenerates. Ryan was permanently and totally blind.

The sniper's bullet had also damaged his olfactory nerve. Unlike the optic nerve, the olfactory nerve can regenerate. The senses of smell and taste come from olfactory receptors, which dangle like tiny strings from the upper part of the nasal passages and pick up molecules in the air. The interactions of the receptors with these molecules are converted into electrical impulses that the brain interprets as smell and taste. Ryan still had a sense of taste, albeit diminished, but no sense of smell.

While at Bethesda, Ryan learned that his SEAL brother and good friend Marc Lee had been killed the same day that Ryan was wounded. Marc had come to Ryan's rescue on the rooftop and risked his life to help evacuate him. After Ryan left the battlefield, new intelligence identified the possible location of the enemy who shot him. When the team was asked if they were willing to return to the fight, Marc was at the front of the line. When they arrived at the target, the enemy engaged them almost immediately. Leading his team up a stairway, Marc suffered a mortal wound. He was the first Navy SEAL to die in Iraq.

There was more bad news. Just like in the biblical account when Job was pelted with one piece of bad news after another, Ryan was hit with what must have seemed like an endless barrage of devastation. Six weeks after he was shot, his SEAL brother Mike Monsoor—his friend "Mickey" from his sister platoon—sacrificed his life for his team. In late September, Mike and his Delta Platoon SEALs were out on their final mission before going home, positioned on a rooftop in Ramadi. Mike was kneeling, looking over a stunted wall, when an insurgent tossed a grenade onto the roof. It hit Mike in the chest and landed between him and his friends. Mike was nearest to the exit and the only one who had a chance to escape the blast safely. Instead, he chose to jump on the grenade and absorb the blast in order to save his friends. He died thirty minutes later. Ryan would later attend Mike's Medal of Honor ceremony.

The loss of these two friends and SEAL brothers was devastating. It was also further confirmation that his survival was a miracle. Through the sadness, Ryan saw hope and opportunity for the future. His life would be a tribute to the memory of Marc and Mike and to Chris Kyle; Luke, his SEAL team commander; Tommy, his medic; the medical staff that worked on him; and others. He was determined to lead others by example; his new life would be a mission.

I believe his experience in Bethesda marked the beginning of a profound transformation in Ryan's life. After being wounded, Ryan experienced faith on God's terms, and just like the Job in the Bible, the challenges were mercilessly thrust upon him. Ryan and his faith would also be tested to see if he could "take it." "But he knows the way I take; when he tests me I shall come forth as gold" (Job 23:10). It's a remarkable irony that this journey started at a place called Bethesda. In the Bible, the healing pools of Bethesda attracted the sick and lame to their waters with the promise that if they washed in them they would be healed. The gospel of John tells the story of Jesus healing a blind man. John said that Jesus "spat on the ground and made clay with the saliva; and He anointed the eyes of the blind man with the clay. And He said to him, 'Go, wash in the pool of Siloam.' So he went and washed, and came back seeing. . . . Therefore they said to him, 'How were your eyes opened?' He answered and said, 'A Man called Jesus'" (John 9:6–7, 10–11).

This gospel passage shows Jesus performing a miracle by curing the man's physical blindness. The story is used as a metaphor to show how faith in Jesus can heal wounds and open one's eyes to a new reality. Ryan Job's transformation began in a place with the same name.

Through his blindness, Ryan witnessed God's love made visible through the SEAL brothers who saved his life on the roof. The medics, doctors, and friends who cared for him in the months following must have appeared as Jesus to him. Jesus healed a blind man in the Bible by opening his eyes. He healed Ryan by surrounding him with people who loved him and were willing to sacrifice for him, people who gave him new opportunities and hope for a bright future. It was all part of an experience that inspired him to live a new life, transformed, full of joy and accomplishment that would honor his fallen comrades and the encouragers who surrounded him.

AN ANGEL

The most powerful force in his transformation, God's greatest gift to Ryan Job, was Amy.

It was another seemingly random event. Ryan and a friend happened to be eating in the same restaurant as Amy and her friend. Ryan was a college dropout who had enlisted in the Navy and was stationed in San Diego with SEAL Team 3. Amy was from the East Coast, a traveling nurse, a graduate of a prestigious Catholic college. The two of them were from opposite worlds at opposite ends of the continent. San Diego was only a short stop on Amy's traveling nurse tour. She planned to be there for a year at most. Ryan had finished his training and was preparing to deploy to Iraq. The universe conspired to bring the healer and the warrior together only weeks before Ryan shipped off to war.

"I knew right away there was something different about her," he told me later. Amy was serious, focused, and disciplined. She challenged him to work harder and set even higher goals. She was twenty-six years old, brilliant and caring, with a bright future in medicine.

The bonds of friendship and affection that they felt in those few weeks before Ryan deployed grew stronger after he was wounded. They had kept in close touch while he was deployed. When Amy heard the news, she took a leave of absence from work and went to be beside Ryan at Bethesda. She was one of the only people who really understood Ryan. As a nurse, she knew it was a miracle he had survived, and she knew his recovery would be long and challenging. She also knew that the physical injury only accounted for a third of the total damage. There were also deep emotional and spiritual wounds that would have to heal.

When Ryan was wounded, Amy left her career and the rest of her life behind to jump into the trench beside him. Together they would fight back, endure some very hard days, and will Ryan back to good health. Amy stayed at Bethesda throughout Ryan's recovery, helping with his medical treatments as well as lovingly working to ease his concerns about the future. In the months that followed, she helped manage, and sometimes led, Ryan's medical care. She knew he would need spiritual renewal, and she would help him on that journey with her own strong, confident steps. Amy had a unique way of firmly weaving her hand together with Ryan's. The lock was deep and full; there were no gaps in the seams of flesh that united them. The grip was so complete that their distinctive hands appeared to be one. It created a powerful, unspoken bond that assured Ryan of Amy's love, and Amy of Ryan's fidelity. Together they looked ahead to the future.

A year after Ryan was shot on a Ramadi rooftop and not expected to survive, he and Amy were married on the beach in San Diego.

"You have to hand it to Amy," Ryan once told me. "She signed up for my blind lifestyle." I've thought ever since then how revealing that statement was about both of them. I thought about the private conversations that Amy must have had with her parents. How did they react to her announcement that she was in love and would marry a blind man? How proud they must have been of their beautiful daughter and how joyful they must have felt over her happiness. I considered their secret anguish and fears as they knew the journey would be a difficult one for her. There are far too many examples of young men coming home from war maimed and disfigured whose wives or girlfriends can't take it. After seeing them and imagining their future together, the women end the relationship or serve the men with divorce papers—sometimes while they're still in the hospital.

Ryan knew his life would be hard. He also knew that Amy had the incredible reservoirs of strength and love to stick with him no matter what. When he arrived at Bethesda, she had no obligation to him. She committed to being his partner for life after he was disfigured and blinded. She always saw past his wounds to the real Ryan underneath, his true character, the part that his SEAL brothers saw, the part that I saw, the part that counted. God had brought them together in his perfect timing to become a part of the intricate fabric that connects us all as part of his plan.

SSITH

During Ryan's recovery, he met many other wounded service members, including Navy SEALs. With two other SEALs who received head wounds, he formed an elite club known as SSITH, which stood for "SEALs Shot In The Head." Their motto was, "This sucks." Despite its limited membership, these three veterans motivated and encouraged each other. It lifted their spirits to know someone else in the world really understood what they were going through. The physical pain was challenging. However, what was even more painful was the realization that they would no longer be fighting alongside their SEAL brothers. At first, the disappointment was so intense that being alive without being able to serve on the SEAL teams must have seemed like a cruel joke. With the help of their SEAL brothers, they learned that although their mission had changed, they were still in the fight—they were still willing and capable of defeating enemies and meeting fierce challenges. But the enemies and challenges were new and different ones.

SEALs pride themselves on never being out of the fight. His fellow SSITH club members lifted Ryan over some very difficult hurdles during his recovery. He never told me their names or how they were wounded. I often thought about how grateful I was that they were there for each other. I had no idea that one day I would become friends with another member of the club.

ARIZONA

An incredible chain of events had directed Ryan Job's life to this point: meeting Amy in San Diego, being spared when an Iraqi trainee manning Ryan's machine gun was killed in Ramadi, and surviving a nearly mortal sniper wound. Another link in that chain placed the newlyweds in Scottsdale, Arizona, a suburb of Phoenix. A nonprofit organization offered them an apartment rent-free while Ryan finished his undergraduate degree. Amy enrolled in a nurse anesthesiology program.

In October 2000, I had moved to Arizona from Boston, where I was born and raised. Eight years later I only kept in touch with a few old Boston friends. Jim, my college room-mate, was one of them. In June 2008, Jim called to tell me his younger brother, Sean, had been discharged from the Navy and wanted to visit Phoenix. He'd never been there before and didn't know anybody, but he just wanted to see the city.

I hadn't seen Sean Carter in more than twenty years. I picked him up from the airport and took him to work with me the next day. Two years before Sean's visit, I had decided to make a career change. After twenty years in the finance indus-try, I felt a tugging need to be more significant in people's lives. I'd taken up competing in Ironman Triathlon races and found that I enjoyed training more than my real job. An Ironman Triathlon consists of a 2.4-mile swim, followed by a 112-mile bike ride, then a full 26.2-mile marathon. All competitors must complete the three-discipline race course in less than seven-teen hours. Training for and finishing an Ironman Triathlon is physically, mentally, and spiritually transformative, and I really enjoyed the process. I resolved to distill the training concepts and mind-set into a consumer program and test my entrepre-neurial skills by starting an endurance training company. My goal was to transform clients from the inside out using my methodology. It was a huge risk and a total leap of faith.

Sean came with me to an early-morning training session. I introduced him as a Navy veteran recently returned from Iraq. Later that day, a woman from the group e-mailed me and asked if Sean knew a SEAL named Ryan Job. The chances were remote. There are more than 320,000 people serving in the Navy; furthermore, Sean didn't know anybody in Phoenix. I asked him anyway.

"You don't happen to know a Navy SEAL named Ryan Job?"

Sean jumped out of his chair. "Yes, I do! We were friends during BUD/S. I lost touch with him when I went to SWCC [Special Warfare Combatant-Craft Crewman]." Sean had enlisted after graduating from college and having a less-than-satisfying experience in the working world. He had reported to BUD/S, and as I mentioned earlier, he entered the front gate with a guy from Washington State named Ryan Job. They became fast friends, a friendship that was made stronger by the fact that they were both rolled back from their original class several times.

The next day Sean and I met Ryan and his guide dog, Trey. Sean and Ryan had not seen each other in five years. In that time they'd both gone to war, lost friends, and come back changed. Now here they were in Arizona together through a series of fateful events, though neither of them had family there. Of all the places on earth he could have ended up, Ryan Job was living fifteen minutes from my house. Even so, had my old friend Jim not sent his little brother to visit me, I might never have met him.

As we sat drinking overpriced coffee, Ryan matter-of-factly told us what happened on the roof when he was shot. Sean and I sat listening in astonishment. He told the names of friends who had died. He showed us his prosthetic eye with the pupil fashioned into a SEAL Trident. Ryan and Sean recounted their time together at BUD/S. When they were about to leave, Ryan said, "Sean tells me you run some type of endurance training company." I said that I did. Then Ryan said a nonprofit group that offered outdoor recreation programs for veterans had offered him an opportunity to climb Mount Rainier, a snow-capped peak more than 14,000 feet high and surrounded by glaciers.

Then he asked, "Do you want to train together?"

That was a challenge I couldn't turn down.

SUPERNATURAL POWERS

Ryan had a supernatural ability to create detailed images and scenes in his mind from verbal descriptions. On Sundays after church he would listen closely to Seattle Seahawks football games on the radio or TV. Ryan loved the Seahawks and had been a loyal fan even throughout all the bad years. Ryan and the Seahawks were a perfect match, as Ryan always rooted for the underdog and he had an amazing capacity to endure pain. He could visualize the game as it unfolded on the field and would anticipate the outcomes of plays. Somewhere in his travels he met Mike Flood, the vice president of community relations for the Seahawks, and on Mondays after the games, Ryan would call Mike and critique the team's performance. Mike is a retired Coast Guard pilot and a veteran whose family has a long history of military service; he and Ryan became good friends. One afternoon Mike put Ryan on the phone with one of the coaches so that Ryan could share his specific recommendations. It's not often that an NFL coach would take recommendations from a blind fan over the phone, but with a record of four wins and twelve losses, what did he have to lose? In early 2009, the team announced they had hired a new head coach. Ryan was disappointed with the new coaching direction, and he predicted that the new head coach wouldn't last a year; sure enough, he was replaced in 2010. The new coach led the team to a Super Bowl victory four years later. Ryan had an uncanny knack for seeing the future.

Chapter Five

MY SIGN

★ ★ ★

MY MOST FREQUENT prayer to God since I was young has been, "Please show me a sign that I'm on the right track, that this is where I should be and what I should be doing." For years I begged, *"Please* just show me a sign so unmistakable that I could not confuse it with anything else but you. God, if you are real, you will show me this sign." Maybe what I'd been asking all along was, "What is my purpose here on this earth?"

When I met Ryan Job in 2008, I was praying hard for evidence that I was going in the right direction. I had left a successful twenty-year finance career to start my company in a new field. It was a complete leap of faith. I had two small children and a wife to support, and my kids had developed this strange habit of wanting to eat every day. My company's clients enjoyed outstanding results, but the business was barely profitable. In 2008, the economy was in a free fall.

I put my worries aside one morning at dawn when Ryan and I were on a training hike up a steep mountain trail in Phoenix. While hiking, I guided Ryan with my hand on his shoulder and with my voice. This particular morning we pushed up the hill together as hard as we could, passing everyone. We reached the top, then turned to come down the same way we had traveled up. The sun had risen, and now the people we'd just lapped could see Ryan's scarred face and closed eyes. They could tell he was blind. Suddenly, without anybody saying anything, they cleared a path for us and started clapping, one by one, all the way down the hill. Everyone clapped and then started yelling, "Nice work!" Ryan asked me what was going on. I didn't want him to know that I was choked up, so I just said, "Keep going. I'll tell you later."

At that moment I realized I'd been asking all those years for a sign from God, and I was walking with my hand on the shoulder of this guy named Job who was leading me down the mountain not by his sight, but by his faith—just like the biblical Job, which, by the way, was about the only Bible story I remember from my Catholic school education. Ryan Job came into my life out of the clear blue, introduced to me by a friend that I had not seen or spoken with in over twenty years, and now he was now hiking with me at dawn in the desert because of my new career leap of faith.

I am skeptical by nature and require neon-like confirmation of everything. God must know this about me, so he manipulated the universe to send a blind guy named Job into my life. He then placed this guy in front of me on a mountain at dawn and had him lead me while dozens of strangers cheered.

You'd think this would have hit me like a lightning bolt, but it was more like a whisper: "Hey, Bob! Hello? You there,

can you hear me now? Can you see it, my sign, the unmistakable one I'm giving you right now? The blind guy leading
you—hey, that's me—that's my sign to you." Yes, God, thanks;
got it, loud and clear. No need for a burning bush.

I experienced God at that very moment and was 100 percent sure of it. At that instant I knew what the philosopher
Carl Jung meant when he said in response to a question about
whether he believed in God, "I don't believe. I know."[1] The feeling was like nothing else I've ever experienced. A wave of relief
washed over me. It was a peace and confidence that I had never
felt before, like I could simply let go of all my expectations and
disappointments. It was like a piece of a puzzle had been put
into place. The puzzle wasn't finished, but there was an image
coming together. While I never felt it from my own father, it
was like my father had put his arm around me and said, "Keep
going. Don't worry, I got you."

This was God's sign to me that I was on the right track, to
just keep going—that he had me covered and he was in control.
His message was delivered to me that morning by a humble,
gracious blind guy, my friend Ryan Job.

A few days later I called to tell Ryan that the people on the
hill were cheering for him.

"They had no idea what happened to you on that roof," I
said. "They know nothing about your struggle or the guys who
never made it back. All they know is that some blind dude just
humped past them on a steep hill."

My voice cracked as I spoke the words, and I could hear his
emotion over the phone as he said, "Yeah. Yeah, I know."

CLIMBING VOLCANOES

A few weeks later, in early July 2008, Ryan traveled to Washington to climb Mount Rainier with a group from Camp Patriot, a nonprofit organization that hosts outdoor programs for wounded veterans. The goal of Camp Patriot is to build trusted relationships among wounded and disabled veterans. The organization considers relationships to be the cornerstone of the healing process, and being tied to one another while climbing a dangerous mountain would certainly build trusted relationships.

At 14,411 feet, Mount Rainier is the tallest peak in Washington State and one of the tallest in the Lower 48. Dangerous snow and ice fields cover its slopes, and the mountain is considered an "episodically active" volcano. This means that the sulfur and steam constantly seeping from cracks at the summit will one day be part of a violent eruption. Confirmation of this future event is clearly visible when you look southwest from the upper reaches of Mount Rainier at the shattered ruins of Mount St. Helens. Mount St. Helens is also an episodically active volcano. It erupted in 1980—one side of the mountain was blown off and fifty-seven people were killed. The episode was the most deadly and economically destructive volcanic eruption in the history of the United States. I understand that for some adventurous souls, climbing an episodically violent volcano may sound inviting; however, this is not really the most dangerous part.

I read a description of the climb to Ryan that stated, "On

average, three people die each year on the mountain, and 50 percent of all climbers fail to reach the summit." Ryan assured me he'd be in the other 50 percent. I have climbed to the summit of Mount Rainier several times and know well the challenges and dangers of the journey. Doing it blind would be insanely difficult, a superhuman feat that I would never attempt.

RUTHLESS CHALLENGES

Ryan had adapted quickly to a life without sight. Like everything else he tackled, he ruthlessly took this challenge without complaining. Being blind is an exercise in humility, as even the simplest tasks require assistance. I came up with a few dignity-saving rituals to make Ryan's life a little easier. I'd always tell him I needed to use the men's room on the way into and out of restaurants. This saved him the awkwardness of asking me to take him. I also ordered our meals, which was easy because Ryan loved anything with bacon. Sometimes I would secretly cut his steak and place it strategically on his plate so he could find it without the agonizing fork-braille technique, which involved moving his fork around his plate hoping to hit a bump of food. Ryan was once a proud Navy SEAL, a true warrior, and now someone had to take him to the bathroom. He accepted this and everything with humor and grace; there was never a hint of regret, self-pity, or anger. He made up his mind that he would be the best blind person in the world, then pursued that goal relentlessly in everything he did.

The daily challenges of blind life would prove trivial compared to climbing Mount Rainier. The mountain is as unforgiving as it is beautiful. But Ryan needed ruthless challenges in his life. It made him feel alive—the harder the test, the more he enjoyed it.

STORM HAZARD

A month before Ryan arrived for his summit challenge, Eduard Burceag, a thirty-one-year-old Seattle engineer, died of exposure while making the same climb. Eduard, his wife, and a friend had set out on a day hike but were caught off guard by a fierce summer blizzard with 70-mph gusts and five-foot snowdrifts. The weather forced them to spend the night on the Muir snowfield, a relatively benign region located on the lower slopes of the mountain. According to officials at Mount Rainier National Park, all three climbers were experienced mountaineers. In fact, Eduard had reached the summit two years earlier. But this time the group got disoriented in the storm. They made a snow shelter, and reports suggested that Eduard had his wife lie on top of him while he hugged her to keep her warm. Shielding his wife from the elements, Eduard became hypothermic and died. After hearing this story, I had some concern about Ryan.

Getting up a mountain isn't the most dangerous part of a climbing expedition; getting down is. At that point, the adrenaline rush of reaching the top has passed and the climbers are exhausted. Many fatalities happen during the descent. In the case of Mount Rainier, as soon as the sun rises, the formerly rock-hard ice starts to melt into slush. Crampons, the spikes strapped onto climbing boots, can't get traction in the soft surface. The downhill trek becomes a nearly out-of-control slide that could end at the bottom of a massive crevasse, which is a crack in the surface of a glacier. On Mount Rainier, the crevasses can be more than 500 feet deep. A slip, fall, or avalanche induced by melting snow can send a group of climbers to an icy grave.

Climbing requires having all five senses fully engaged at every moment. At night, freezing and shifting ice creates a symphony of growls, whines, cracks, and pops. It's vitally important to know the location of moving ice, as it's a predictor of new hidden crevasses on the climb route. A sniper's bullet had robbed Ryan of his sight and his sense of smell. Smell is a key asset on the mountain. Not only does it alert a climber to morning coffee and hot food, it warns of potential dangers: propane gas leaks from portable stoves or the damp ocean scent that precedes fast-moving mountain storms. These storms are another treacherous challenge to mountaineers. The moist smell is a signal to move fast and find cover.

THE CLEAVER

Ryan and his guides would travel the most direct route to the summit, a line known as the Disappointment Cleaver route. A cleaver is a rocky, steep outcropping that separates two glaciers. On Rainier, Disappointment Cleaver divides the

Ingraham Glacier from the Emmons Glacier. Disappointment Cleaver is a nearly vertical, very narrow, very slippery trail. There is no room to pass, and conditions deteriorate rapidly as the sun melts the ice that restrains loose rocks. Falling on the Cleaver leads to one of several outcomes. One is the climber smashing over rocks before landing at the bottom of the Cleaver. This is the good option. The other two options are far less attractive. They involve climbers falling over either side of the Cleaver, leading to a quarter-mile tumble, slide, and roll before sliding to a stop either embossed into the glacier or lying deep inside it. When Ryan and I talked about this, I told him I did the math and suggested it would be best for him not to fall. Ryan agreed and then complimented me on my keen analytical skills.

Mountain climbing is a team sport, both safer and more fun in groups of three or four. Climbers wear harnesses that wrap around the legs and waist. Harnesses are connected together by a rope. Thus, if one climber falls, the others keep him from sliding or tumbling down the mountainside. However, it can also happen that the one who falls drags the whole rope team down the mountain. It's a curious situation in that you're either each other's saviors or downfall.

Downfall was the outcome on the afternoon of June 11, 1998, when an avalanche swept twenty-seven people down the Cleaver. Early summer is particularly dangerous for avalanches, as rising temperatures melt the winter snow. One of the survivors remembered, "I heard people screaming 'help,' screaming that they were cold, screaming that they were going to die. At the end, it was like tumbling bodies and they just kept going."[2]

Patrick Nestler, a twenty-nine-year-old novice climber, ended up dangling by his rope 100 feet over the edge of the Cleaver, injured but alive. The afternoon sun melted snow into freezing water that ran off the Cleaver and onto Nestler. Soaked and helpless, he dangled over the rocks and ice for seven hours as rescuers worked frantically to save him. By the time they finally pulled him to safety, he was dead of hypothermia.

Excited as Ryan was about the climb, he was not cavalier about the risk. Rather, he was excessively cautious. He told me that he climbed by taking short, fast, probe-like steps while using his hiking pole to poke a semicircle pattern in front and beside the area where he would place his foot. He said he could feel the general direction of travel from the tugging of the harness rope. "I locked in on the crunching sound created by boots and crampons biting into the hard snow a few feet in front of me and tried to put my foot into this track," Ryan explained. "It was mentally and physically exhausting."

On July 7, 2008, Ryan started out from the Paradise Visitor Center at 6,000 feet with a large support group assembled by Camp Patriot. The horde included two other wounded veterans, professional mountain guides, a CNN journalist, Keni Thomas (a former Army Ranger turned country music star), a team of Microsoft employees who volunteered to lug extra gear to base camp, and members of the Army's Fifth Special Forces Group, who climbed above the team to stand watch over their warrior brothers and offer support. The caravan moved skillfully up the Muir snowfield. Ryan wore his 60-pound backpack. For this stage of the climb, he wore no rope or harness. His guides, Curtis Fawley and Art Rausch, positioned themselves in front of and behind him. They tapped with their poles and shouted directions: "Big step, step six inches left, now forward two steps . . ." Ryan used his touch-and-listen method for six continuous hours over a four-mile stretch, climbing from 6,000 to 10,100 feet. He arrived at Camp Muir exhausted but totally unassisted. As Curtis, his guide, said, "He made it look easy."

SUMMIT BID

Camp Muir would be the staging point for Ryan's summit attempt. Muir is a bustling base camp for mountain guide services. From there the guides shepherd their clients to and from the summit. The site separates the lower mountain with its majestic snowfields from the steep, glacier-covered upper mountain. Every step beyond Camp Muir would be confirmation to Ryan that he had not been defeated—that the past no longer had a hold on him. He was wounded, but not broken.

The team set up tents, ate, and slept, or tried to. Sleeping at 10,100 feet in the bitter cold with two other people in a tiny tent pitched on an uneven slope, with only a thin piece of fabric between you and the freezing, rock-hard ice, is not as sexy as it sounds. One of the most challenging aspects of mountaineering is sleeping, or more accurately, not sleeping. Uncomfortably not sleeping.

There's also the issue of relieving oneself, which means dressing in warm clothes for a cold march to the outhouse facilities, of which there are several. These sturdy rock and plywood structures are a welcome oasis from the cold and wind, and a far better alternative than having to go in the great outdoors. Ryan was grateful for all of it and perhaps much better suited to handle the situation than the others. He slept only a few hours a night at home and often needed to be led to the bathroom. None of this was different at Muir. Also, the same husky build that protected him from the chilly Pacific surf during SEAL training insulated him here as well, and he could carry the heaviest of packs uphill forever.

The next day Ryan and his team spent the better part of the morning in climbing school on the glaciers around the campsite. This is where they learned to self-arrest, essential ice axe skills, and other techniques. After school, the group ate, hydrated, and rested in their tents, mentally preparing for their summit bid. By ten o'clock that night, July 8, 2008, the mountain was once again cold and hard. That was when Curtis Fawley, the lead guide, "knocked" on all the tents to deliver the message they'd been waiting for: "Saddle up! It's time to climb a mountain."

Adrenaline surged through Ryan's body. He layered his clothes, wiggled into his climbing harness, and strapped on his crampons. He was ready. Curtis was a veteran guide with more than 125 summits on Rainier. He connected his rope to Ryan's harness and positioned Ryan between himself and his other guide, Art Rausch, a retired Army major, firefighter, and seasoned Rainier guide with more than two hundred summits. Curtis and Art were the most experienced guides on the mountain. Once again, Ryan was surrounded by a hedge of protection.

At 11:30 p.m., the team started out from Camp Muir toward their next objective, Cathedral Gap. Cathedral Gap is a bowl-shaped section leading up to the base of Disappointment Cleaver. One entire side of the bowl is a 500-foot-high ornate rock face that bends inward over climbers traversing below; this dome structure resembles a natural cathedral. Passing through the area, climbers get the uneasy feeling they're being watched by the stone monolith towering over them. Dozens of rocks and boulders shave off of the face daily and plummet into the gap like a primitive bowling alley, with the climbers as pins. The rocks roll to a stop, leaving trails in the snow on or near the climbing paths.

The day after Ryan and his team passed through the gap, a fifty-year-old climber crossed Cathedral Gap in the late morning—the worst time to travel because the sun melts away the ice holding rocks that have shifted overnight. He was hit in the face by a baseball-size rock and had to be airlifted to a hospital. Having all five of his senses didn't save that climber from danger; at the wrong time of day, Ryan would have been easy prey for the Cathedral's shrapnel.

After two and a half hours, Ryan and his guides arrived at the base of Disappointment Cleaver. Taking on the Cleaver is a bit like getting married: if you're not 100 percent sure, don't do it. It is possible to turn back, but doing so will most certainly be a costly disaster. Turning around is insanely dangerous, especially in the dark. The path is steep, narrow, and covered with loose rocks and ice. The climbers' spiked metal crampons created sparks from the weight and friction as they slipped and slid over rocks. Ryan's group had a solid head start over other climbers headed for the summit. However, below they could now see dotted strings of head lamps punching through the darkness. In the black night, other groups of climbers, anxious for their summit, were moving up fast. Ryan had to get up the Cleaver promptly.

The team knew the Cleaver was their biggest challenge. Curtis, Ryan's lead guide, reeled in the rope separating them so that they were only three feet apart. Art was locked into Ryan from the back, giving him verbal directions. The three traveled as one unit in a curious waltz for two continuous hours all the way to the top of the Cleaver. Curtis and Art tightened their hedge of protection, whispering encouragement as Ryan struggled to scale the route. "I was on fumes when we exited the Cleaver," Ryan later recalled, "and we still had 3,000 more vertical feet to go."

Four hours into the climb, the team took its first extended rest break on Ingraham Flats, just above Disappointment Cleaver. It was 3:00 a.m. on July 9. Rest stops are almost as much work as climbing. Scaling the mountain generates a huge amount of heat, so climbers are constantly managing their temperature by putting on and taking off clothes. They get dehydrated more rapidly at higher elevations, so it's essential to drink on each break. Climbers burn nearly twice as many calories as normal because they're using energy both to keep warm and to move up the steep slope. Ryan was burning more than 1,400 calories per hour. After four hours of climbing, he had already shed a pound and a half of body weight.

As the team relaxed on Ingraham Flats, they were unaware of the eleven climbers buried beneath them. In early June 1981, a group of climbers and guides were resting in the same area when a huge wall of ice broke off and crashed down on them. Eighteen people escaped. Ten climbers and one guide were swept into a 100-foot crevasse, then buried by 70 feet of solid ice. Their bodies were never recovered. Danger is an ever-present companion on the mountain.

The rest stop was just long enough to recharge and prepare for the next push up to the high break at 13,000 feet. The thin, rarefied air had far less oxygen than at lower altitudes, making it difficult to breathe. Going forward, the team would have to employ the rest-step technique they learned at climbing school the day before. This is a simple but effective technique that resembles slow-motion rocking. The technique conserves energy and allows for rhythmic pressure breathing, which helps to keep oxygen in the lungs.

The team pushed on and arrived at the final rest stop just after sunrise. It was 5:30 a.m. They had been climbing for six and a half hours. Ryan felt the warm sun on his face. He noticed the different sound the crampons made when they dug into softening snow. He felt the thinness of the air more with each hour of climbing. Others on the climb could see the lights of Yakima, Washington, in the distance. At 13,000 feet, they could look down and see the scattered clouds covering the Cascade Mountains below them. The summit was within reach, a mere 1,411 vertical feet away.

Ryan's confidence and excitement grew as the team made their final push for the top. It was here that all our disciplined heart-rate zone training would pay off. In the weeks before his climb, Ryan had transformed his cardiovascular system to become highly efficient at converting oxygen and stored body fat into energy. While many of the other climbers looked down and gasped while their hearts pounded vigorously to pump as much oxygen-rarefied air to their lungs as possible, Ryan trudged up the final stretch with a grin on his face as his heart pumped steady with a hum like a powerful diesel engine!

Strong winds near the summit make it impossible to hear. Voices get carried away with the airstream. Curtis now had to lead Ryan from the front with a short, tight rope while Art kept him centered by tugging left or right on his rear rope. There was no room for error. A slip and fall now could launch the trio thousands of feet down the mountain. The upper reaches of Mount Rainier are littered with bottomless crevasses. Ryan and his guides were forced to weave their way around and over huge ice fissures before they could reach the summit.

It was near 8:00 a.m. on July 9, 2008, less than two years after Ryan cheated death on a rooftop in Ramadi, when he stood on the rooftop of his home state of Washington: the peak of Mount Rainier, Washington's tallest and the fifth tallest in the United States outside Alaska.

While at the top, the climb team unrolled the Seattle Seahawks Twelfth Man banner that Ryan's friend Mike Flood had entrusted him to carry to the summit. The Seahawks fans are so loud that the team refers to them as their "twelfth man." The noise level in the stadium has registered 137.6 decibels, which is just slightly above the level of an F-15 jet taking off. The Seahawks permanently retired the number 12 as a tribute to their fans. The twelfth man is this unseen force that motivates everyone on the team to play at a higher level. Ryan was the embodiment of this unseen force; he made everyone around him better. At the summit Ryan smiled proudly behind the Twelfth Man banner of his beloved Seahawks.

The team spent less than an hour on the summit before packing up to return the same way they'd come. The trip was slow and dangerous, a controlled slide in some areas. It took almost as long to get back to Camp Muir as it did to reach the top. The team returned exhausted but elated. They would spend the night at Muir reviewing the accomplishment of the day. The next day they would continue on down to Paradise Visitor Center where they had started the climb three days before. On the morning of July 10, 2008, as Ryan prepared for his final descent of the mountain, he heard the distinctive rumble of fighter jets in the distance. Camp Patriot had arranged for two F-15 fighter jets to buzz directly over Ryan to acknowledge his achievement. "It felt like they were three feet over my head," he remembered. "I could feel their roar in my chest. It was an amazing experience."

At their triumphant return to Paradise, Ryan and the others were greeted by a large group of family, friends, and well-wishers. *Seattle Times* reporters were there to capture the story and take photos. The feature published in the paper on July 11 carried a photo of Ryan hugging his grandmother as he arrived at the finish. The *Times* story reads in part:

> A sniper's bullet in Iraq in 2006 took Ryan Job's sight, but not his grit, his determination and his love of the outdoors.
>
> All three were in evidence as the 27-year-old former Navy SEAL from Issaquah became one of three current or former servicemen, severely injured in Iraq, to reach the top of Mount Rainier on Wednesday with the help of volunteer guides. . . .
>
> Job, who hiked and backpacked often in his youth but never considered climbing Rainier, said that even without sight, he could sense the majesty of the 14,411-foot peak, especially approaching the summit.
>
> "You can feel the altitude. Everything feels bigger. Everything feels open. There's no sound except the wind. The air is crisper, colder, and you feel like you're on top of everything." . . .
>
> Job . . . was roped to as many as three guides at once during the most dangerous part of the climb. On a normal ascent, climbers have as much as 20 feet of rope between them, but with Job, guides were roped just 3 feet away, using the tension on the rope to help signal him where to step.[3]

EARNING BACK DIGNITY

Reaching the summit of Mount Rainier allowed Ryan to earn back the dignity he had lost to blindness. It was confirmation that he would continue to lead a fulfilling life. However, the summit was not just for Ryan. It was for Chris, Luke, Tommy, Marc, and the others who came to his rescue.

SEALs as a group are not prone to talking about their feelings. Their emotions are expressed in powerful and unmistakable actions. Reaching the summit of Mount Rainier was Ryan's way of telling all his SEAL brothers, "Thank you," and "No need to feel sorry for me." To each other, these actions demonstrate love, respect, and gratitude.

Ryan knew that Chris Kyle blamed himself for not being the target when the sniper's bullet struck. Chris was extremely protective of Ryan. Ryan wanted Chris to know that he was grateful to Chris for risking his life to save him. He needed to show Chris that blindness was really no big deal, and he could more than handle it.

Ryan wanted Luke to know he was a great leader who made the right decisions all the time and that Ryan was honored to serve with him. He was grateful to Luke for his friendship and for risking his life on the roof. He wanted Luke to see that he had indeed gone on to accomplish worthy goals despite his blindness.

Ryan needed Tommy to know he was brilliant. It was Tommy's deep sense of compassion and disciplined self-study that afforded him the skills to help save Ryan's life.

And Ryan wanted to honor Marc Lee. Marc's actions had spoken loud and clear: when asked if the team wanted to engage the enemy who shot Ryan, Marc Lee was the first in line. He gave his life while pursuing the enemy who shot Ryan.

Ryan's summit was also to honor the medical professionals who worked to save his life, some of whom risked their own lives.

These SEALs had all seen dead and wounded, but not one of their own until Ryan was wounded. That was when the war became personal. Ryan was the first SEAL to be severely wounded in Iraq. Marc was the first SEAL to be killed there. In the years following, many more would be killed and wounded. Ryan once told me he was glad he was the one who was shot because he could handle it. He said that somehow he knew he was not going to die and that this was all part of a bigger plan. That morning on the roof altered the destiny of all their lives.

Chapter Six

TRANSFORMATION

WE ALL HAVE the ability to transform from who we are into who we desire to be. This is our true destiny. How is it then that some of us, like Ryan, achieve our destiny and fulfill our dreams while so many others live in frustration, yearning for more, regretting the past, and repeating the same mistakes over and over again?

We all believe in our own individual greatness: that we can be more, achieve more, and become more successful than we are today. This type of transformation requires a totally new belief system. How then do we change? We can't change by doing more of the same. Doing the same thing over and over while expecting different results is what Albert Einstein called insanity.

But is there a formula for change that we can all follow, something that will keep us from repeating the same mistakes over and over again and lead us to our own greatness? I believe the answer is yes, and the formula is simple. But not easy.

The formula requires us to do what is uncomfortable and unfamiliar. We all resist this. Change is much like training for a marathon. At first running seems painful and uncomfortable, but over time, as the miles add up, the body and mind become conditioned to running. At some point running becomes enjoyable. You know that a change has occurred when the very things that were once uncomfortable and unfamiliar become comfortable and familiar. True transformation requires a combination of pain, persistence, and faith. Combined, the three enable us to overcome our past, the naysayers, and critics. Pain, persistence, and faith are powerful enough to override even our own negative self-talk and difficult circumstances. And finally, this transformation trifecta allows us to overcome ourselves to become someone totally new.

Pain is often the trigger for change, persistence is the engine, and faith is the fuel. Without faith the entire process grinds to a halt. Pain starts the process, persistence puts change in motion, and faith carries us across the uncomfortable chasm until one day our efforts pay off.

Ryan changed, and the evidence of his change was sprinkled all over his life. There was once a time when he really hated running, and he mentioned this to me as we lugged a treadmill that he had purchased into his apartment so he could do his daily run training.

AMAZING GRACE

John Newton employed this formula and experienced a truly remarkable transformation. Like Ryan Job, Newton was a sailor. He was a ship's captain and a slave trader. Sailors of his day had a reputation for being foulmouthed. Newton, by all accounts, set new standards in vulgarity, and even by a sailor's criteria he was considered revolting. His nickname was "The Great Blasphemer." That is, until a raging storm engulfed his ship. The storm seemed like a curse, relentlessly tracking and battering the ship for eleven days straight. The sails were ripped to rags, and the planking along one side of the hull was completely torn away and splintered.

The crew had little hope of survival. Many died, but the survivors worked furiously at the pumps in a last-ditch effort to keep the vessel afloat. After he became too exhausted to pump, Newton fastened himself to the wheel in hopes of steering the sinking ship to safety without being swept overboard. For eleven desperate hours he fought to hold the ship on course against impossible odds.

Tied to the ship's wheel, surrounded by destruction, and facing certain death, John Newton examined the wreckage of his own life. It seemed as if it was as ruined as the decrepit ship he was trying to steer through the storm. He remembered his mother's prayers that he would become a minister and the scriptures she had taught him as a child.

It has been said there are no atheists in foxholes. One of my friends who is a hardened Navy SEAL can attest to this fact. He shared with me that during his last firefight in Iraq, as he lay dying in a shallow ditch after being shot in the face by a machine gun, he could hear his wounded enemy in a trench just yards away. His enemy was calling to Allah while he was imploring God for the strength to live as the life drained out of both their bodies.

Newton's foxhole was the helm of that ship, the merchant

vessel *Greyhound*. There's nothing quite like the fear of impending death to change a person's thoughts and belief system. That day at the helm, March 21, 1748, Newton was transformed.

It was not his approaching death that frightened Newton into change; it was instead his painful acknowledgment of his wretched life. He saw that it was not God who had put him in grave danger aboard the *Greyhound* but his own thoughts, actions, and beliefs.

Newton decided at that moment to make a trade. He would completely toss away the familiar, comfortable habits of his old life—the foul language, rogue associates, quick temper, and selfish ways—and embrace a new life. During that storm he found a Bible and began to read. He let go of all the horizontal relationships in his life and invested wholly in a vertical relationship with God.

Each of us is the product of our lifestyle, which is a series of habits or behaviors strung together that we cling to day after day. Our behaviors are the products of our beliefs. Those beliefs are products of our thoughts, which can be strongly influenced by the people, events, and environment around us. So does that mean we're nothing more than the product of our environment? Are the outside world and our horizontal relationships with others controlling the inside of us? If that's true, then how can we hope to change and fulfill our dreams and destiny?

The raging storm allowed Newton to experience faith on God's terms. He survived the storm and eventually gave up slave trading. His persistent and faithful study of the Bible reinforced his faith and new way of thinking. Newton revered the Bible not simply as a religious document but as an owner's manual and a guide for human transformation. He made his vertical relationship with God his priority, then aligned himself with like-minded people—their mutual support was like steel sharpening steel.

Newton was onto something. In his book *How God Changes Your Brain*, neuroscientist Dr. Andrew B. Newberg documents the physical changes to the brain as a person contemplates God. Dr. Newberg conducted brain scans of people who practiced contemplative forms of focused prayer and meditation, revealing a marked decrease in parietal lobe activity. He observed that the decrease in activity "allows the mediator to feel at one with the object of contemplation: with God, the universe, peacefulness, or any other object upon which he or she focuses."[1]

In another study of the thalamus, the "Grand Central Station" of the brain, Dr. Newberg called the changes "most unusual."[2] The thalamus plays a critical role in identifying what is real and what is not. In subjects who had meditated consistently for fifteen years, one side of the thalamus was lit up while the other side was dormant.[3] "For advanced meditators," Dr. Newberg reports, "this asymmetric reality becomes their normal state of awareness; God, tranquility, and unity becomes an integral part of their lives, no longer a thought but a palpable experience, as real as the book you are holding in your hand."[4] It's curious that the "palpable experience" of God—tranquility, peacefulness, and unity—are exactly what

Paul described as the "fruit of the Spirit" and evidence of a Christian lifestyle in Galatians 5.

This modern brain scan evidence could be used to argue that John Newton was actually *physically transformed*. It was not an act. However, what is truly amazing is that Newton's own mind and thoughts, which are not part of the physical brain, likely actually changed areas of his physical brain. Thus, in a sense God performed brain surgery on Newton, changing his brain without ever touching a scalpel.

The prayers of John Newton's mother were finally answered. At the age of thirty-nine, Newton began a forty-three-year career of preaching the gospel. In his diary on March 21, 1805, fifty-seven years after his stormy transformation, he thanked God for the painful storm when he wrote, "I endeavor to observe the return of this day with humiliation, prayer, and praise. Only God's amazing grace could and would take a rude, profane, slave trading sailor and transform him into a child of God."[5]

Like Job in the Bible, and Ryan, Newton thanked God for the storm that nearly took his life. You may know John Newton by the famous hymn he wrote, "Amazing Grace." Its lyrics are known the world over:

> *Amazing Grace! How sweet the sound*
> *That saved a wretch like me.*
> *I once was lost, but now am found,*
> *Was blind but now I see.*

RESPONDING DIFFERENTLY

Suffering, pain, and loss are all a common part of the human condition. Thus, we all have the opportunity to experience profound transformation as a result of it. Uncommon reactions to these common conditions make us uncommon, rare, and exceptional. Ryan embraced his condition after being wounded. His constant refusal to be a victim fueled his determination and inspired everyone who met him. The hardest part of the transformation formula is having the faith to act with courage in the face of suffering and pain.

Chapter Seven

LOOKING FORWARD

★ ★ ★

RYAN JOB'S CONTINUING transformation made him a legend in the eyes of everyone who knew him. On his dining room wall was a framed letter from President George W. Bush with his SEAL team's photo below it. The personal letter thanked Ryan for his service to the nation.

We were training together for an Ironman Triathlon, and he was representing the wounded veteran community at events across the nation. One day he was dropping the puck to open the NHL hockey season, and the next he was speaking to business leaders at a chamber of commerce luncheon. On top of all that, he was in school full-time and worked part-time at General Dynamics C4 Systems in Scottsdale.

All the traveling meant a lot of time in airports and on airplanes. Ryan and I had a standing agreement that I would be his transportation to and from the airport in Phoenix. Not that he needed any charity from me—far from it. Be it training or going to the airport, Ryan made his blindness an adventure for both of us.

He never acted like he was blind. When speaking to others, he would approximate the location of their eyes from hearing their voices and try to make direct eye contact with them. The only giveaway was his guide dog, Trey, who had SEAL-like discipline to complement Ryan's—including the ability to "hold it" for six hours while lying by Ryan's side.

There were times when Ryan seemed to know where we were going better than I did. One day I took Ryan and Trey to the airport for a trip to New York, where Ryan would be the guest of honor at a Navy SEAL Warrior Fund dinner. Amy was in the middle of exams, so only Ryan and his canine sidekick were going. As we walked through the terminal, Ryan suddenly asked, "What terminal is this?" "Three," I answered. "We need to go to four," he said, turning around and heading back the way we'd come. I followed, feeling a little sheepish.

BLIND INTRODUCTION

In New York, Ryan was met by his old commander, Luke, who escorted Ryan off the roof in Ramadi. He was now escorting him and Trey through the evening, introducing him to the various well-wishers and dignitaries. One of the attendees seated at Ryan's and Luke's table was a smart, confident, beautiful television news anchor. Trey sometimes pushed the boundaries of his guide-dog role and was vying for the attention of the his female table guest. Ryan used the opportunity to chat up the young lady. Later that night Ryan introduced her to Luke, a Naval Academy graduate, who was built like an NFL linebacker and whose Texas accent made him sound like Matthew

McConaughey. The two of them exchanged contact information. As Ryan told me when he got back, "I did my part. Trey and
I got Luke a date with a hot TV news anchor."

Ryan and I were on a long run when he filled in some more
details about Luke.

A few weeks after Ryan arrived in Iraq, their team was
assigned a high-profile rescue mission. A young prince was
being held hostage by Al-Qaeda in Iraq. As intelligence came
in, the team stayed busy training, preparing, and reviewing
assignments.

"There's a ton of work that goes into executing these ops,"
Ryan explained, "and Luke had a way of making sure we were
all totally focused. Word finally came down that the mission
was a go. It's really exciting and stressful, like the moment
before the kickoff of a football game. We were all jocked up in
our battle gear, loaded into our Humvees with engines roar-
ing, ready to roll out. The air support had already launched."

Ryan was sitting behind Luke's seat as Luke walked toward
the vehicle. Just as he was about to climb in, the intel guy
ran out of the plywood shack that served as the intelligence
office and handed him a piece of paper. The intel guy, whom
Ryan remembered was "just a kid," said that new information
showed there may be dug-in machine guns around the com-
pound, IEDs, and booby traps.

Luke didn't even break stride. He took the paper, folded
it, and put it in his pocket. Then with his calm, confident
Texas accent, Luke looked the kid square in the eyes and said,
"Thank you. I appreciate the info."

The team arrived at the target to find no machine guns, no IEDs, and the prince up on the roof with a bunch of women and goats. They secured the boy and delivered him back to his family.

"Do you know why Luke didn't hesitate or change his plan?" Ryan asked me. I thought about it for a long while. Why would a commander not tell his men about newly discovered risks? Then it dawned on me. Luke must have already anticipated these possible hazards and more, then woven them into the team's preparation.

"Exactly!" Ryan responded. "He was an awesome leader. Totally dialed in." He added that Luke's command and the Navy also saw his unique talents, and he was later given a special assignment to develop and train the next generation of Navy SEAL leaders.

I always found it curious how Ryan and Luke became such close friends. Luke was Ryan's SEAL team commander senior officer, many years older than Ryan. Luke's officer responsibilities would naturally distance him from Ryan and the other enlisted men. Years later I came to know Luke and understood how he bridged the gap to become highly respected by the men that served below and above him. Luke accomplished this by standing beside, behind, and in front of his men. When bullets were flying and men were dying, Luke was standing in the middle of it all, leading his men, pushing and pulling along with them; he humbly gave them all the credit for success, and he encouraged them after some very hard days. Because of this, Luke's men bestowed him with authority. As Ryan put it,

"I would gladly follow Luke to hell and back." Authority is the currency of all great leaders. Luke understood that authority is earned, not given, and he earned it from his men and from the senior command. Luke inspired loyal followers who became the engine of his influential leadership.

Chris Kyle, who served directly under Luke, paid him one of the greatest compliments any leader could receive: he once said, "I loved our new commanding officer. He was outstanding, aggressive, and stayed out of our hair. He not only knew each of us by name and face, but he also knew our wives and girlfriends. He took it personally when we lost people."[1] Chris would never know how true and important those words would later become.

BLIND HUNTING

In October 2008, Ryan was traveling again. This time he was off to Idaho to go elk hunting with Luke at Camp Patriot. In the car on the way to the airport, I pointed out that he was blind, and that in most cases hunting required seeing your prey. I also suggested he may not want to mention his condition to other hunters. "You know how hunters are," I said. "Some may find it a bit unsettling that a blind guy would be pointing a loaded gun at targets he couldn't see."

Ryan grinned. "Relax. Micah, Luke, and I have it all figured out." Micah is the executive director of Camp Patriot. Then Ryan said, "How do you like your elk, burgers or chops?"

Though he'd been an avid hunter before he was wounded,

Ryan had never hunted elk. He and Luke talked about going elk hunting together when they got back from Iraq. One of Ryan's greatest disappointments in becoming blind was that he would never again stomp through the woods for hours on end stalking prey with his friends. Hunting, for Ryan, was a chance to get away. He was in it for the sport, not just the meat. Some people enjoy a good book on a white sandy beach. Ryan's idea of relaxation was being cold and wet on the side of a mountain downwind from a deer the size of a dump truck.

On his Mount Rainier climb, Ryan happened to mention to Micah that he and Luke bemoaned the fact that they'd never get to hunt together after all. Micah and Ryan had talked in July. By October, Micah had made arrangements for Ryan and Luke to fly to Idaho and meet him at one of the nation's premier big-game hunting ranches.

The ranch was several hundred acres of rolling hills, meadows, and woods where animals were allowed to breed and roam free within boundaries marked by high fences. Elk were harvested by hunters who paid tens of thousands of dollars for the opportunity. There was a butcher on staff and a meat processing facility on-site so that nothing went to waste. "The entire experience is far more humane than mass slaughter of farm animals," Ryan explained.

Micah solved Ryan's problem of "seeing" by mounting a tiny Internet video camera on Ryan's rifle scope, which fed a real-time image to a laptop computer screen that Luke was watching. Luke could see the crosshairs of the sight and whatever game was downrange. It was like a video game with real bullets.

Though blind hunting is not novel, many so-called blind hunters are not actually blind. Rather, they're legally blind or visually impaired. Ryan had an issue with the definition. "Call me a purist, but I'm blind," Ryan declared. "I'm missing an eye and can't see out of the other one. They can see light, shapes, and colors. We're not talking semantics here. I once saw stars when I walked into a low-hanging tree branch, but other than that my world is totally black. The criteria should be that if you can drive yourself to go hunting, then you are not blind."

As soon as they arrived on the ranch, Ryan and Luke set out to stalk a massive bull elk. They spotted one, set up downwind of the beast, and waited. As the elk walked across their location, Ryan centered the zero on the perfect spot. Luke, whose eyes were glued to the video screen, ordered, "Now!" Two days after I had shuttled him to the airport, Ryan called to let me know Micah's video rifle worked. He and Luke bagged a 980-pound giant elk with a rack over five feet tall. He told me his blindness was his advantage because the elk underestimated him. I never did.

SLEEPLESSNESS

Working out with Ryan was fun. We had a special interval routine we did at his apartment: pull-ups, lunge jumps, push-ups, burpees, and a 1,000-meter row. We did our best to turn each other "inside out"—to see who would get sick first. He was a fierce competitor and loved to push the pace. In this, as in everything else, Ryan considered blindness an inconvenience rather than a disability.

We also ran together. Most blind runners hold a cord looped like a fan belt while their workout partner holds the other end. We both found this system cumbersome. Ryan was not a fast runner, but he could hold a steady pace. If he could hear my feet and knew where my body was, he could run beside me without any attachment. With that in mind, I developed a novel approach for us to run together. I showed up one morning to run with little bells on my running shoes. Listening to the high-pitched jingle I made with every step, Ryan asked, "Did you step in fairies?"

I could tell he was uncomfortable with me walking around attracting attention by the sound of little fairy bells on my shoes. We tried it once but couldn't manage to increase the pace beyond the beat of "Twinkle, Twinkle Little Star."

The next training session I changed out the shoe bells for my two-year-old son's little maracas carried in my pockets. They worked perfectly, keeping the pace while allowing Ryan to sense my location. They were also more subtle than bells, a shaking sound with more of a Caribbean feel.

We went on long runs, sometimes for more than two hours, in a walk-jog-run-walk pattern. These were great sessions, time away from everything and everyone to think and talk together. We talked about politics, business, and being married. We discussed the future, school, and life in general. Sometimes we talked about the war.

Our workout intensity would depend on Ryan's recovery. Since his return from Iraq, he'd had trouble sleeping. He would go weeks at a time on a few hours of sleep a night. Doctors had ruled out any physical problems, and sleep medication made him groggy for days. After weeks on end of sleep deprivation, he would finally crash, sleeping for twenty-four hours straight or longer. Sleep deprivation is debilitating and can cause memory loss, hallucinations, slurred speech, blackout, dizziness, and more.

The body's natural circadian rhythm—the "clock" that tells a person when to eat and sleep—is thrown off balance in a blind person. Since Ryan's world was totally black, his body was deprived of the natural signals for going through a daily rhythm. Sleeplessness is also a telltale sign of posttraumatic stress disorder, or PTSD. But Ryan was not convinced that PTSD was a real condition with physical symptoms, nor was he willing to accept the idea that he might suffer from it.

His SEAL friend Chris Kyle said, "There's no way you can go in, kill people, see people blown up and maimed and everything, and not come out with some stress."[2] However, he acknowledged that PTSD was "hugely frowned on" by most SEALs. I absolutely understood why Ryan rejected PTSD or a stress response alone as the cause of his insomnia. Ryan didn't have a "disorder"; he was fully capable, accountable, and highly functioning. Maybe he rejected stress as the cause because it was something inside of him but outside of his control. I am sure that many people's first reaction to the diagnoses of certain illnesses is disbelief. They can't believe that their body has conspired against them.

I reasoned that Ryan had been under a constant state of escalating stress that peaked when he was wounded. Now his blindness had thrown off his circadian rhythm. In a strange way I was relieved by my amateur diagnosis because if Ryan hadn't been deeply affected by war, then he might really have a problem.

The PTSD stress response can be triggered by powerful memories. The emotional attachment to the memories is so strong that it can cause the same chemical reaction as the actual event. My thought was that if a body could be trained into this constant state of stress, then it could be trained out of it. I came up with a plan. If Ryan's stress trigger was the emotional charge attached to his old memories, then we would defuse those memories by creating new, more powerful ones.

I decided to test this theory in our regular training sessions. These sessions left Ryan emotionally defused and physically exhausted. We discussed details of his war experience that replayed in his mind. This process worked for us because we trusted each other. It wasn't a matter of him divulging military secrets to me; it was a matter of us not passing judgment on each other. I told him that I would not hold his past against him if he would not hold my past against me.

In one of our sessions, I told Ryan that after college I worked as a staff assistant for a US senator who was extremely liberal. My job was to resolve constituent cases involving veterans and military service members, and I was proud of my accomplishments and still had many of the thank-you letters I received. Ryan was a conservative, and not one of those moderate Tea

Party bleeding-heart types—he was a proud ultra-conservative and thought militias were a little too liberal. So you can imagine how stunned he was at my confession. He looked down and shook his head side to side in a wordless no. After a long pause he looked up at me and said, "I would have never guessed." He didn't hold it against me—eventually.

As he shared his experiences, Ryan had to translate all the military acronyms and jargon into civilian-ese, which required a lot of objectivity and detailed descriptions. I just listened, sometimes for hours, and asked a few questions to help me better understand the circumstances as we examined the wreckage together. He wanted me to understand that he had no regrets about being wounded, and that his SEAL team's courage and leadership were the reasons why he made it out of Iraq alive. Ryan wanted to clarify that Marc Lee gave his life protecting other Americans. "Americans were still out there, at risk. Marc was protecting American lives. The only right decision was to go back out. I am sure that more Americans came home because of Marc's sacrifice."

Ryan and I finally just accepted that war makes the irrational seem rational and the perverse seem normal. I appreciated how Ryan explained this alternative universe to me. I have never been in the military and never claimed to understand what he experienced. But he introduced me to some of his demons, and a few of them kept me up at night too. We didn't try to rationalize the what-ifs of the past. We just sorted it all out.

Years later I was again reading the book of Job and realized that much of the book describes Job's conversations with his friends. The biblical Job confided in his friends too. Job's friends attempted to rationalize and justify Job's suffering, which seemed only to make his suffering worse. As I read the exchange between Job and his friends, it occurred to me that Job really wasn't looking for suggestions or answers to his problems; it seems that he just wanted to share some of his burdens with people he trusted.

Over time I could feel Ryan's emotions drain out of the events as he described them to me. Soon his memories seemed to lose their charge. They were more matter-of-fact. He pointed out lessons learned as he educated me in various strategies and tactics. His memories took on a tone of wisdom. Maybe that's what wisdom is: the experience without all the emotion. We gradually moved on to other subjects like climbing high mountains and Ironman Triathlons that we would do together.

To be candid, I don't know if our approach worked or not. I like to think that he slept better at night, but I had no way of measuring any change in his internal clock or his autonomic nervous system. And besides, he was my friend, not my patient. What mattered is that we enjoyed the process and we trusted each other. We had worthy goals and specific targets.

Our training continued. Together we figured out how to run, bike, and hike as one unit, and we became great at it. The sessions with Ryan were the highlight of my day. Each of us made up for what the other lacked; together we were greater than the sum of our parts. Each day we became more optimistic, confident, and hopeful about the future.

These were tough times. Ryan was working hard to overcome his wounds and move on with his life. I was struggling to keep a company afloat. The Great Recession of 2008 had cost millions of people their jobs and their homes. Wars were raging and people were dying. There was a heaviness that accompanied each new day. Despite all this, Ryan and I were empowered. We had plans for the future and pursued them together. Looking back, I think we could all use a little empowerment like that all the time.

TREY

Ryan gained independence through his dependence on his guide dog, Trey. He was a beautiful, sensitive, highly intelligent creature. Former Secretary of Defense Donald Rumsfeld made Trey available to Ryan through a donation to Southeast Guide Dogs. Back in 2006, when Ryan was wounded, there were few programs for wounded military personnel to acquire service animals. Now there are a number of outstanding programs that match service animals to wounded veterans.

Trey was a purebred black Lab with legit AKA papers to prove it. He had brown fur on his chest, legs, and eyebrows and looked exactly like a Rottweiler save for his long tail. Ryan insisted that he was a purebred black Lab, but then again Ryan was blind. People would ask, "What type of dog is he?" Ryan would say something to the effect of, "A black Lab. But one in every 3 million black Labs has a latent gene that expresses unique brown coloring. It's a leftover vestige from the breed's ancestors, who were used to hunt timber wolves."

It's possible that Ryan made it all up just to mess with people. Ryan was like that. But it sounded plausible, and Trey looked the part.

Trey wasn't just handsome; with his magnificent square head and broad chest, he was elegant to the point of looking regal. He was the quintessential canine version of a Navy SEAL. Trey's destiny, his very purpose in life, was to be a guide dog, a highly disciplined fearless protector, and a loyal friend. He was Ryan's new "swim buddy," a term used in BUD/S training for a person assigned to look out for another. Ryan said that during BUD/S, swim buddies were never, ever allowed to be out of each other's sight. Trey would keep a close watch on Ryan, lying under his desk while he was studying and sleeping at the foot of his bed. Trey trained years for this mission; he was in peak physical condition and ready to serve. Ryan and Trey were a perfect team. Trey could open any door, and when he did he would come prancing out of the room with a big grin and his tongue hanging out, mocking everyone. He sensed where Ryan wanted to go and would be out front, pulling Ryan toward his intended objective.

Guide dogs are trained to communicate through the harness and handle—the "pull" communicates various types of information to the owner. Ryan told me that he weighed 193.2 pounds after a haircut and blowing his nose. He was a big body for anyone to pull. Ryan would grab on to Trey's handle, and Trey would tilt forward, squint, dig in, and give a potent yank on the handle. Then he'd guide Ryan from point A to point B. Trey was all business on the harness.

Chapter Eight

MANLY SHOPPING

★ ★ ★

RYAN AND I needed to find a birthday gift for his wife, Amy. Arizona is nuclear hot in August, and the night brings little relief. The blazing sun heats up the ground, and a heavy, low layer of humid clouds traps the heat. It's so hot and humid you can actually see rain falling in the distance, but it evaporates before it hits the ground. People joke about the dry heat in Arizona, and it is dry, except in August—when you need a set of gills to separate the water from the air.

The annual late-summer monsoons that bring an end to these conditions hadn't arrived yet, so the daytime ground temperature was over 100 degrees. Trey didn't make the shopping trip with us because his feet would have burned on the asphalt under those conditions, and his thick fur coat was not appropriate Arizona summer attire.

Like most men, Ryan and I shopped from a list and didn't deviate from it. No freelancing whatsoever. If we couldn't find an item, we quickly moved on to the next item on the list. Ryan's list had exactly two items: (1) a travel pillow, size large; and (2) lavender massage oil. Ryan had already done the recon and mapped out our targets. The objective was to hit Brookstone first for the pillow, followed by a short trek to The

Body Shop, where we would secure the massage oil. A simple, straightforward mission, fifteen minutes tops.

Since Trey was not with us, I would be Ryan's guide. I found it faster and more efficient to do this like we did on our mountain hikes, my hand resting on his far shoulder, communicating directions with my voice and hand signals. A push equals straight forward, a shoulder squeeze means stop, my palm pushing out signals move outside, and my fingers pulling inward reads move inside. Ryan was okay with this system on mountain treks, but not so comfortable using it in a crowded mall. He thought it came across as a public display of affection, which we both disliked, no matter who was doing it. He insisted that the "proper method" was for him to reach out and touch my arm while we walked. "Both methods look like public displays of affection," I told him. "Your 'proper version' is just more awkward." My method allowed us to talk and walk together at the same pace. We moved at such a quick and agile tempo that it was impossible to tell that Ryan was blind. The only giveaway may have been Ryan's sunglasses, but in Arizona everyone wears sunglasses in the mall.

It took only a few minutes to get to Brookstone and secure item number one: travel head pillow, size large. With 50 percent of our mission complete, we were off to snag item number two from The Body Shop. We navigated across the mall, my hand on his shoulder, smiling and laughing as we entered The Body Shop. I instantly noticed the woman behind the counter studying us with a bashful grin. I squeezed Ryan's shoulder as we reached the counter, and at the same time I realized I was about to ask the woman where we could find the lavender massage oil. I considered the implications of this question and thought to myself, *Why couldn't Amy have asked for something less complicated, like a trip to Hawaii?*

I opened my mouth, but nothing came out. There was an uncomfortable pause as my mind raced. The lady at the counter just smiled and stared right back at us. "What's wrong?" Ryan asked. "Is somebody looking at us?"

I thought about saying, "They're closed," and turning around. He would have never known the difference. We could have bought something different, but that would have meant going off the list, and we didn't know how to do that. Besides, we were already inside the store, standing at the counter.

Finally I said in my most diplomatic, formal tone, "Not that it matters in any way whatsoever, but I just want to clear something up before we start. My friend here is blind, and I'm helping him with the purchase of a gift."

Ryan held up his left hand and flashed his wedding ring, chiming, "Yes, we're married." She looked at us with a puzzled stare. I added, "But not to each other. He's married to Amy, and that's who the gift is for. Anyway, can you please show us the lavender massage oil?" She led us to the right section and handed us a few samples, asking Ryan if he wanted to smell them. When he said no, the woman handed the bottle to me. "Do you want me to put a test spot on your hand?" I asked Ryan.

The woman gave me an odd look. "He can't smell either," I explained. "This one's fine." We paid, I put my arm around Ryan, and we walked out of The Body Shop together.

Neither of us said a word until we reached the car. Then Ryan turned to me and said, "You're not my type. And besides, you're ugly!"

"I feel the same way about you!" I shot back. Ryan had been blind for two years before we met; he'd never seen my face.

BIG NEWS

Shopping mission accomplished, Ryan suggested a late lunch at his favorite Italian eatery. He seemed really excited; I thought it was because of the lasagna. Ryan loved to eat. He would dissect his favorite meals with technical descriptions like a professional food critic. The minute the server left with our order, Ryan blurted out, "I have some big news, but I can't tell you. You have to guess."

"Can you at least narrow it down?" I prodded.

"Amy's pregnant!"

"Just give me a hint," I said. Ryan couldn't keep this secret to save his life. "Wow, that is awesome! Congratulations!" Ryan was beaming, so proud he could hardly contain himself. He said his brother's wife was pregnant too, so he was going to be an uncle and a father all at the same time. There was going to be a lot of diaper changing in his future. It was the perfect job for him because no matter how bad it looked or smelled, he could handle it. I had known Ryan for more than a year at that point. We'd spent a good deal of time together, and I had never seen him that happy and excited.

"I really haven't told anyone," Ryan continued, "so don't say anything. Amy made me promise."

"Did you tell Luke?"

"Yes."

"Chris?"

"Yes."

"Your brother?"

"Yes."

"So you already basically told everyone?"

"Yeah, basically. Except that Amy doesn't know that I did."

As a SEAL, Ryan had endured the military Survival Evasion, Resistance, and Escape course, training for weeks under stressful conditions. He endured simulated torture in order to learn to resist divulging sensitive information if captured. But it only took his baby to make him crack.

BIG-HEARTED AND COMPLEX

Ryan was complex—he was big-hearted and caring but also resolute and direct. He once e-mailed me an audio clip of a television news interview he gave after a group of Navy SEALs rescued the captain of the *Maersk Alabama* tanker ship. Pirates had taken the ship and the captain hostage off the coast of Somalia, Africa. The story was later made into the film *Captain Phillips*, starring Tom Hanks. A team of Navy SEAL snipers shot and killed all but one of the hostage takers, who had placed themselves and their hostage in a desperate situation. Ryan told the TV reporter, "Despite what your momma told you, violence does solve problems."[1] I understood exactly what Ryan meant—there was no diplomatic or political solution to the crisis, and allowing pirates to take American vessels and crews hostage would set a bad precedent in other parts of the globe. Weeks before, in fact, the pirates had killed other hostages. Ryan's statement was in no way meant to be bravado; he was merely conveying the fact that many times violence brings about a successful conclusion to a hostage crisis. The SEALs spoke the only language that the Somali pirates understood: violence. Apparently, the SEALs' response acted as a deterrent, since the Somali pirates have consequently stayed clear of US flagged vessels. Chris Kyle later turned Ryan's statement into a patch he wore on his hat.[2]

FORGIVENESS

One day I asked Ryan about his family back in Washington. He had a younger sister and said he and his younger brother were very close, but he didn't communicate much with the rest of the family. I told him that I loved my parents and siblings, but there were times that we just did not get along. We concluded that every family has its degree of dysfunction.

I could sense this was a tense topic that was really drawing him backward in life. I'd been there myself. I offered a simple solution. "Forgive them," I said. "Forgiveness is not just for them, it's for you. Who cares if they don't accept it, deserve it, or want it? Lift the burden of anger and frustration off your shoulders and move on. Forgiving them takes away all the drama, which takes away any power they have over you. You've evolved and been transformed—forgiving them proves this."

I continued, "Whatever happened, whatever they did or said, let it go and move on. Don't get me wrong. Forgiveness and trust are two very different things. Those who forgive and forget are setting themselves up for a life of frustration. You should forgive, but it's best not to forget, because the person is prone to do it again. True change requires a revolution in a person's entire belief system. Most people aren't able to understand this, much less do it. Revolution means you abandon, trash, and throw out your old ways of thinking, speaking, and doing and replace them with new behavior that is altogether different. So you have no obligation to forget but for your own sake you should forgive."

I then shared my favorite Mark Twain quote with him: "Forgiveness is the fragrance that the violet sheds on the heel that has crushed it." We've all been heels at some point in our lives. I told Ryan I had been the heel too many times and was now committed that for the rest of my life I would be the violet's fragrance. Ryan seemed delighted by this concept and willing to apply it.

Ryan had changed. He was different, and other people noticed. Ryan was engaged in a personal transformation. There was an aura of calmness about him. It seemed that other than his relationships with Amy and his friends, the things of this world had little hold over him. He seemed to have a much bigger mission. Ryan was patient, tolerant, funny, and always positive. I would see more evidence of his change in the months ahead.

THE MOST DANGEROUS WORDS

Ryan shared with me that he felt his greatest skill was the ability to out-suffer anyone. This was embedded into Ryan's DNA. Ryan suffered and struggled. His transformation took place when he responded to his own suffering in a different way. He no longer thought about and reacted to events in his life as he had in the past.

As I mentioned before, I believe pain and suffering are part of the human condition. We can choose to be transformed by it or be victims of it. Victims cry, "Why me? Not fair!" They blame others and pray for the storm of suffering to stop. Victims eventually become bitter and offer others no lessons, no inspiration. They take away and drain from, rather than giving to and lifting others up. Ryan refused to be a victim, even on the roof after being shot. He insisted on walking on his own so his team members wouldn't have to put down their weapons to carry him. He declined to let blindness hold him back. And what was even more impressive was that he would not let his blindness be an excuse for anything short of excellence.

Being shot is a very personal experience. The enemy chose Ryan, even as there were many other targets, both on the ground and on the roof. The sniper had a killing hierarchy that would have made Chris Kyle his primary target, yet he settled on Ryan. Ryan and I pondered the irony of this in the context of the story of Job in the Bible, where the enemy also selected Job. In the book of Job, God spoke the most dangerous words in the entire Bible when he said to the enemy Satan: "Have you considered My servant Job?" (Job 1:8). The devil himself was looking to torture someone in order to test that person's faith, and God offered up Job. With this, Satan "tests" Job by taking all his possessions. The devil is sure that Job will rebuke God, but the devil is wrong. Frustrated with Job's unwillingness to give in, Satan then layers Job with sores from head to toe, and kills Job's children. Job's wife is horrified and presses Job to "blaspheme God and die!" Job responds by scolding her for cursing God. Ryan and I had a good laugh at this because God allowed everything to be taken away from Job, but he left him with one thing: his demanding wife. "I'm glad God has our sense of humor," Ryan declared.

God knew that Job was the only person on earth who could handle all the torture and pain with dignity and grace without cracking. Ryan knew he could handle it too. He told me that he felt so fortunate he was the one who was shot; he felt that all the good that came into his life because of it far outweighed the bad.

Those who have been transformed make peace with their suffering and pray for the strength to make it through the storms in their life while others beg for the storms to end. The transformed become enlightened by the process. They think beyond themselves, beyond their own pain. They have a confidence wrapped in humility. Ryan chose to be objective about his suffering, which is an amazing feat. While he had low periods and some very bad days, he leveraged his suffering to develop a personal, more trusted relationship with his wife, his friends, and his God. Ryan's survival was a miracle. It was as if God intervened, just like in the story of Job. God protected Job and restored his health.

PART THREE ★★★
REDEEMED

Chapter Nine

A DIFFERENT WAR

★ ★ ★

UNKNOWINGLY RYAN WENT from fighting the war in Iraq to fighting a different, more crucial war. Many who accept Christianity have no clue that as soon as they do, they're enlisted in a conflict. A conflict that rages every second of every day. One that competes for our heart, mind, and soul. To fully live the Christian adventure, we have to turn off the TV, stop living in denial, and refuse to participate in the tit-for-tat, one-upmanship lifestyle that society demands we should engage. Christians are called to act differently from their past and differently in response to others.

Ryan would not allow the outside world to control the inside of him. The outside world expected Ryan Job to become a victim, to be bitter over the loss of his sight, to lash out and blame others for his circumstances, and to lament being wounded. The outside world labeled him disabled and blind. To Ryan these labels were used to lower expectations of him, to make excuses for him, to make his wound greater than him. Ryan refused to be a prisoner of these labels; he rejected all of them. Ryan placed his faith in a loving God and fought against the temptation to become a victim. There were some very tough days, weeks, and months, but God sent Ryan his guardian angel, Amy. Her hand firmly clasped in his as she whispered words of empowerment was more than enough to reinforce his faith.

The instant one becomes a Christian, one also becomes a warrior. The essence of Christianity is love, which is constantly under attack, thus the war. God knows that we won't win every battle. The flesh will overpower us from time to time. Still, he encourages us to stay in the fight. He said the tangible evidence that we are on the right path would be the fruit of the Spirit: "love, joy, peace, forbearance, kindness, goodness, faithfulness, gentleness and self-control" (Gal. 5:22–23 NIV). Our victory is the fruit, and God's victory is us, his redeemed.

The spoils of victory were evident in Ryan Job's life. He had a loving wife and loyal friends; he was gracious with his time and talents. Ryan didn't win every battle, but he would eventually win the war. Ryan's transformed life was God's victory. In a strange way, Ryan's struggle helped us both understand and accept how God works. In his blindness Ryan saw a bigger picture; he didn't major in the minor. The minutiae of life —travel delays, long lines, bills, the archaic health-care system that he endured—were of little concern to him. He took it all in stride. He yearned for relationships and spent time with friends; that was where he would apply his wisdom. It was subtle. He never lectured or gave advice—he simply lived his faith, all in, all the time, in spite of his struggles. He never thumped a Bible. The evidence of his faith was in things he did not do or say. I don't think I ever heard him curse. He was always grateful.

Although it was clear to me that Ryan embraced a Christian lifestyle, the one time he gave me any verbal evidence that he was a Christian was when I asked him what type of music he listened to. He replied, "Country and Christian." Ryan offered subtle clues to his faith. Once in an e-mail describing his blindness he wrote, "I am now totally blind in both eyes for the rest of my life on earth." Only a believer would choose to end the sentence in that manner. Years later Ryan's brother would reveal to me, "Ryan wasn't always that way." I took this to mean that he did not always fully invest in his faith. Ryan's transformation was not from a bad person to a good one or a faithless person to a faithful one; Ryan was always a good person. His transformation was more profound than this. It was from a casual observer of faith to a fully engaged, unfettered participant in faith. Trusting that God had a plan for him was Ryan's only safety net. Ryan's transformation meant that he was no longer counting on self-confidence and his own abilities to get him through life. He joined together with God and placed his faith and confidence in him. This type of faith transformed Ryan's life from ordinary to extraordinary. He was working hard to live as Jesus taught, full of forgiveness, courage, and trust in the power of God's plan.

Ryan was confident and humble and lived his life as an example rather than making excuses. Most of all, he was a great friend who was always willing to help, and he was more interested in my life, my happiness, and my success than in his own.

SURGERY

In late September 2009, Ryan was scheduled for yet another surgery. This one was to restore blood flow to the area below his right eye so that bone and skin grafts applied in a previous procedure would continue to heal. This was one of twenty or so operations that Ryan had endured since being wounded. There is no such thing as routine surgery. I knew each operation was hard on him and on Amy, but Ryan took them all in stride.

Ryan had made many trips to California and other places for evaluations by various specialists and for more surgery. He and Amy endured the surgery intervals together, like professional athletes preparing for an away game. Amy took care of all the travel plans, consulted with hospital staff, and ensured that his follow-up care and medications were in place. She was the head coach; Ryan was her star athlete. She had been by his side since the week after he was wounded, observing, questioning, and nursing him back to health. She was an experienced nurse who was studying to become a nurse anesthetist, and she was the foremost expert on her husband's injury.

Whenever Ryan traveled or Amy needed a break, Trey would spend time with my family and me. I arrived to pick up Trey one Sunday night to find Ryan relieved that he had just posted the last assignment of his undergraduate career. He and Amy sat together as he told me he would graduate the following week. I congratulated him and gathered Trey's leash and toys. Ryan would go to the hospital in the morning for pre-op tests.

For reasons I couldn't articulate, I had a bad feeling about this surgery. I tried not to come across as apprehensive, but Ryan could sense my uneasiness, and he would have none of it. He stood and told Trey to be a good boy and told me we'd be back in training soon. Then, for the only time in our lives, there in his living room I hugged him and told him I loved him. Amy smiled and said thanks.

OUR PROMISE

Ryan arrived at Maricopa County Medical Center on Monday morning, September 22, 2009. He would undergo two major vascular surgeries: one on Monday and the other on Tuesday. The initial procedure was to harvest a vein from his leg and implant it in his head. The second operation was unplanned but not unexpected: Ryan's surgeon had to reopen the head area to repair a leak in the newly implanted vessel.

I spoke to Ryan after the first operation, and it was the only time he ever confided in me that he was in pain. I had seen Ryan push himself beyond the breaking point in our training sessions. He had suffered through his climb of Mount Rainier, the torture of BUD/S, and being shot without saying a word about pain. But on the phone that day he was almost in tears, saying, "I'm really hurting right now." Even so, he thanked me before he hung up.

The second operation on Tuesday was a success. I talked to him late in the evening after the procedure. He was still in pain but lucid, his speech slightly slurred as he told me that he was excited to get home and get on with life. He was full of questions about Trey, our training schedule, Amy and the baby, and my family. I told him that he should get some rest and that I would be over the next day with Trey to visit. "Just relax," I said. "I will take care of business here. You just take care of business up there." It was late, after ten thirty at night. I could feel him smile as he said thank you and good night, and we both hung up the phone.

MY KING

At five thirty the next morning my cell phone rang, and Amy's number appeared. My heart rate spiked. I could feel my heart pounding in my throat and the blood rushing through my body. I answered and knew immediately from the pain in her voice that something was very wrong.

"Why?!" she cried. "This can't be happening, this can't be happening!" She was hyperventilating.

I kept Amy on the phone while I quickly dressed, jumped in my car, and rushed to pick her up. She and Ryan's mother, who was there to visit, were waiting for me at Ryan's apartment. We were all in a state of confusion, panic, and shock. I prayed that there had been some mistake or mix-up. I had spoken with Ryan just six hours before. I drove us as fast as I could to the hospital. We arrived at the entrance to find some hospital staff members waiting for us outside. I drove past them into a parking space. The look on their faces confirmed the unthinkable: Ryan was dead. I got out of the car and took Amy and her mother-in-law's hands, now a widow with an unborn child and a grieving mother. In a daze, we walked together through the sterile hospital halls to face the news. Together we stood in the hallway outside Ryan's room, where a doctor met us and said calmly, "Ryan passed away early this morning."

Sometime in the early-morning hours of September 24, 2009, my King came to take Ryan home. He picked Ryan up in his arms, held him tight in a loving embrace, and whispered in his ear, "There is no more pain, no more fear, and no more darkness. You have passed every test. You are victorious, and you are redeemed. You are home now with me, where you belong." And my friend Ryan was gone, just like that. Years later, as I write these words, my eyes still fill with tears.

REDEMPTION

The word *redemption* has a number of meanings, and each one could apply to a different stage of Ryan's life. There is *redemption* defined as "to extricate from or help to overcome something detrimental." This meaning would apply to Ryan's redemption from the bullet wound that nearly killed him. His redemption was made possible by his SEAL teammates who rescued him from the rooftop, and then the medical staff in Iraq and Bethesda who put him back together.

Redemption's second meaning is "to change for the better." Ryan's eyes were opened at Bethesda, where he and Amy became one and set off for a better life. Ryan told Amy a few weeks before he died that his priorities in life were his faith in his Savior, Jesus Christ, followed closely by Amy, and then his SEAL brothers, family, and friends.

Finally, the word *redeem* means "to win back." God's victory was Ryan Job. After being wounded and accepting Christ's love, Ryan's life was blessed beyond what he could have ever imagined. The story of Job in the Bible tells of a reward for his faithfulness. Ironically, this reward was also true for my friend Ryan Job: "The LORD blessed the latter days of Job more than his beginning" (Job 42:12).

This life that we all have been given is an amazing event in the history of the universe. For a short time, we will walk the earth together and commune with others, and when our work is done here, our Creator will take us home. Believing in the Redeemer is the final victory for every Christian. Along the way we will not win every battle, but victory comes to believers at the moment of their death. Ryan's relentless faith made him victorious both in life and in death. He won the war. Because of this, Ryan was God's victory.

THEY LIED

My last conversation with Ryan was replaying loudly in my head: "I will take care of business here. You just take of business up there." I didn't know at the time that it would be a promise for life. Ryan needed me now more than ever. His widow and unborn child were counting on me too. But for what?

We stood in the hallway outside Ryan's room. The hospital staff and Ryan's surgeon seemed stunned and could not give us a clear reason for the cause of death. I asked if we could move to a room to sort it out.

Amy sat in a chair, inconsolable, and the staff stood surrounding her. They offered speculation and what I perceived as an outright lie as to how Ryan died. They told us that Ryan's death was because he aspirated chewing tobacco. I knew instantly that this was not true. Ryan was working hard to give up the habit because he knew Amy hated it. All of Ryan's friends, including me, were his tobacco suppliers. We would drop off tins of fine-cut chewing tobacco to him when Amy was at school. I would randomly go by to pick him up for coffee so he could enjoy a dip while we planned our training schedule. We had all seen him use it; he would place a small pinch between his lower lip and gum, but you had to look close to detect it. He would often swallow some, and it never bothered him.

I left the room, pulled a nurse aside, and asked some simple but direct questions. I started with, "Why didn't anyone respond to his monitor alarms?" Patients are fitted with a host of monitors and sensors that alert staff in the event of a sudden drop in blood pressure or loss of heart-rate signal.

The nurse noticed that I had turned from mourner to accuser and said in a slightly arrogant tone, "He was a difficult patient and kept removing his monitors."

"Let me understand this. Your hospital policy is to allow blind patients—who have just undergone not one but two major vascular reconstruction procedures in less than twenty-four hours and are heavily medicated—to remove their own monitors?"

She said, "You need to talk to my supervisor."

I asked why someone didn't check on Ryan. I was told that someone checked on him at midnight, then again around 3:30 a.m., when they found him "unresponsive." It was a surreal situation. He had survived BUD/S, his SEAL team hazing, and a sniper's bullet, but it was a hospital in Arizona that killed him. I was infuriated that hospital staff and doctors could insinuate, especially to his widow in that awful moment, that somehow Ryan irresponsibly killed himself. I was positive that the medical staff in that room knew that someone in the hospital, perhaps someone in that room, maybe the nurse I spoke with, had killed Ryan. He did not aspirate on chewing tobacco. I could feel it; my entire body was shaking with anger. They were all lying and trying to cover up something. I was sure of it.

Ryan was there under their care because of the wounds he received in war—he was awarded the Bronze Star—and they checked on him once. Meanwhile, our enemy prisoners of war held at Guantanamo Bay are monitored by military guards twenty-four hours a day, seven days a week. I was so angry, confused, and hurt, but I needed to stay focused for Amy's sake. I made a promise to Ryan, and he needed me now.

I asked to see him and was led to room seven. I noticed the room was directly opposite the nurse's station and outside the room there was a crash cart, a defibrillator on wheels.

I asked the nurse for some privacy and shut the door behind her. The room was gray, and florescent lights glowed down on Ryan, lying motionless in his bed. There he was,

Navy SEAL, hero, pilot, mountaineer, son, brother, husband, father-to-be, and my friend. His face was emotionless, his skin pale, his hands by his side. He was dead. Ryan had cropped his hair off prior to going into the hospital. A foot-long crescent-shaped wound, closed with about a hundred sutures, extended all the way over his head from his left ear to his right. I forced myself to touch him. There was still a tube in his mouth from when they tried to revive him. I opened his mouth to search for any signs of chewing tobacco, and then I inspected his hands. They were by his sides, his nails well trimmed and his fingers cold and clean.

I then inspected his bed. The sheets were tucked in around him. I pulled to release them and saw on his right thigh, slightly above his knee, a white rectangular bandage covering the incision where the vein had been harvested to reinstall it in his head. The bed was clean and neat, and there were no signs whatsoever of tobacco. Ryan's brand of chewing tobacco was a fine cut that looked like a cross between oily tea leaves and dirt, and it had a strong mint odor. The smell was as unmistakable, as penetrating and pervasive as gasoline. If he had aspirated on chewing tobacco, there would have been evidence somewhere. There was none.

Just as I finished examining him, his cell phone rang. It was in his bag on the floor beside his bed. I opened the bag and searched frantically until I found the phone at the very bottom, next to a full tin of chewing tobacco. The hospital lied! They made up the whole chewing tobacco story! My mind raced. I could feel the blood draining from my head like I was going to faint. "Please, God, please," I prayed. "Please tell me what to do. I need you now."

I left Ryan's room and walked directly into Ryan's surgeon. He had seen me with Amy earlier. He stuck out his hand to introduce himself. He looked stunned and confused. "If there is anything that I can do—" he began.

"Do you know who you killed in that room?" I demanded. Before he could answer, I continued. "He was a highly decorated Navy SEAL who survived a hellish battlefield wound that left him blind. This is not good, you know."

The doctor looked frightened. I knew in my gut what had happened: someone had killed Ryan, most likely by a deadly cocktail of incompetence and arrogance. I turned and walked down the wide sterile hall, not knowing where I was going, praying over and over, "Please, God, please just tell me what to do right now. I need your guidance and help. Please, God, tell me what to do."

At that moment I felt a sense of composure and peace. It was the same feeling I had when Ryan and I were hiking that day and the people started applauding. Then a clear voice spoke in my head. It was my own voice that seemed to be coming from someone else. "Call Rob." Rob Dunaway was my business attorney, and he always gave great advice. It was 7:45 a.m. when I called Rob and he miraculously answered his phone. I explained what happened. He knew of Ryan. He told me to stand by and he would have another attorney get in touch with me soon.

Ten minutes later, Buddy Rake called me. He said that he

was a Navy veteran and had handled many of these situations. Buddy Rake would soon join the hedge of protection around Ryan. He suggested that I make a request in writing for each and every medical record related to Ryan's care, then call the coroner's office and request a full autopsy on behalf of the family. I wrote down everything on a piece of white paper in large, clear letters as he spoke, and then I repeated each task back to him. I was not going to relegate these unfamiliar tasks to mental notes.

I got off the phone with Buddy and called directory assistance for the number of the coroner. I told the woman who answered that I wanted to speak to the coroner directly to request a full autopsy. She told me that the protocol for a full autopsy was at the discretion of the medical examiner. Then she asked, "Is the deceased Ryan Job?" Apparently the hospital had already called it in.

I told her that yes, it was Ryan Job, and gave her more information about Ryan and what I had experienced at the hospital. In the background I could hear her change locations and close a door while I spoke. She listened, then said, "I will make sure that your request is documented and given every consideration." I think that she too suspected something was amiss. She said that she was sorry for my loss. I thanked her and crossed the item off my list. I made sure to complete both tasks that Buddy assigned to me at the hospital. I submitted Amy's signed copy of a medical records request form to the hospital staff, gave a copy to Amy, and kept one for myself.

I told Amy that I knew she was pregnant and that Ryan

had told many of his friends. She asked me who else knew. I told her everyone and that Ryan was so excited to be a father he just couldn't wait to tell us. She was concerned about the baby. Then, in one of the most dreamlike events of my entire life, Amy, an ultrasound technician, and I went into room five, while Ryan's body lay in room seven. I met Ryan's daughter for the first time, a beautiful little life beating inside her mom. I saw her heart beating, and I knew right then that God's plan was in motion.

FABRIC OF SUPPORT

As word got out, Ryan's friends arrived at the hospital. Ryan's supervisor and another colleague from General Dynamics were the first ones there. Ryan had recently secured a full-time job at the company. The real estate agent who arranged for Ryan's apartment arrived along with Ryan's friend Wynn Tyner. The only person Amy asked me to call was her pastor, and soon after my call, Pastor Jamie Rasmussen and another pastor arrived from Scottsdale Bible Church, where Amy and Ryan attended Sunday services. In the first weeks after arriving in Arizona, one of Amy's priorities had been to find a church. Each week she drove herself and Ryan to Sunday services. Together they sat, hands clasped, in the front left pew, where Ryan concentrated on the message delivered by Pastor Jamie, the son of a lawyer. Ryan listened as Pastor Jamie delivered his sermon like a skilled attorney arguing a case on behalf of a Christian lifestyle. He explained the currency of the Bible and made lessons relevant to Ryan's daily life. Jamie's words and ideas made sense to Ryan and advanced his transformation.

The hospital was soon teeming with people from the community who made up a fabric of support and formed a hedge of protection around Amy and her baby. Amy's parents arrived in the early afternoon. Her mom was fighting breast cancer at the time. Ryan had shaved his head in solidarity with her. I'm sure Ryan never knew the irony of his act compared to Job's in the Bible. Job did the same thing in solidarity with the suffering and loss of his family: "Then Job arose, and rent his mantle, and shaved his head, and fell down upon the ground, and worshipped" (Job 1:20 KJV).

Amy's father led Amy with her unborn child, her mom, and me into Ryan's room. We all joined hands, and Amy's father prayed over Ryan, an honest, compassionate prayer that gave thanks for Ryan's life. He asked God to bless his soul and to give us all the strength to carry on.

I later came to believe that perhaps the purpose of Amy and Ryan's seemingly random meeting was to help lead Ryan to a deeper faith. Ryan once told me that Amy was "different." I know now that the difference was her faith. Amy's family was an intellectually superior crowd. Her dad was an MBA, her brother was a PhD, and she was a nurse anesthetist. Yet what made Amy different was not her intellectual prowess but her anchor of faith. Her faith allowed her to live simultaneously in two different worlds: a secular world where faith was often treated as an accessory, like a handbag used during special occasions, and her other world where faith was at the center of her life. Amy never mentioned it to me, and like Ryan, she never thumped a Bible, never invited me to church. She just lived her faith all in, as best she could, all the time.

On the cruelest day of her life, Amy asked only for her family and her pastor. In the following days I witnessed Amy's faith in action during what had to be the hardest, most stressful time she could ever imagine. She was unfailingly gracious and resolute. When people ask how she ever managed to get through such a terrible time, I believe that I know how. It was her faith. That was the rudder that directed her course. Amy's faith made the invisible visible: as a believer she manifested God. There is no feigning faith in times like these. A person's strength is in equal proportion to his or her faith. Amy leaned on the trust that God's plan was in motion and Ryan's passing was part of it. And this belief leaned back at her, like two friends seated with their backs pressed against each other, propping each other up without effort. Amy made God real to me by her courage reinforced through faith.

Ryan's diploma and grades came in the mail the same day he died. He graduated with high honors and a 4.0 GPA.

Chapter Ten

THE SEALS

★ ★ ★

BEFORE WE HAD even left the hospital, almost every Navy SEAL on the planet had heard of Ryan's death. News travels fast in the SEAL community through a highly efficient network of relationships. It is a single organism with tentacles that reach around the world from boardrooms to operating rooms to battlefields. Ryan's passing sent a wave of shock, disbelief, and sorrow through the organism. A part of it had died, never to be replaced and never to return. It was now time for SEALs to honor their warrior brother, care for his family, and be a pillar of strength for his wife and unborn child.

Chris Kyle arrived at Ryan's apartment first, a day before his old team leader, Luke. The Navy issued orders for Ryan's SEAL brothers to rendezvous in Arizona from battlefields and training sites around the globe. They would all come and surround Amy with a hedge of protection. All day, every day, the SEALs were at her side, to grieve with her and to get through the next second, minute, hour, day, year, life. It was amazing to see this brotherhood arrive en masse to honor one of their own. They accept death; wakes, funerals, and burials are all part of the business of war. Their sorrow for the loss of their brother was tempered by the pride they had in his character. He was part of them and they were part of him—their DNA had been mixed through years of training, fighting, bleeding, drinking, freezing, sweating, winning, losing, suffering, and dying together. They would not cower at his loss; rather, they raised their brother up with honor. Together they acknowledged his greatness and his sacrifice. Together they remembered him as their warrior and proudly buried him like a Navy SEAL.

The Joint Special Operations Command dispatched a young Army officer to be the military's liaison to Ryan's widow. The woman had known Ryan and Amy for years as their advocate and guide through the maze of military procedures and medical paperwork required for Ryan's care. The major was stoic and professional. Bereavement was her occupation; over the years she had helped lay to rest too many warriors. She had seen the shock and disbelief of shattered families as they forced themselves to go through each agonizing step of burying their sons, fathers, brothers, and husbands. Ryan's death weighed heavily on her; it drained her. She did her best not to show it, but her eyes betrayed her. The horizontal lines that traveled the length of her upper lids were heavy; grief filled and pushed down hard. She was tired but soldiered on with incredible tact, immersing herself in the task of planning Ryan's funeral.

Luke arrived late in the evening. He had been in Iraq and traveled more than thirty hours straight to get to Arizona. He was coordinating orders for Ryan's old platoon to arrive in Arizona. Luke's arrival put things in motion—he quietly took the lead. Amy leaned on him for decisions and support. Chris was right when he said, "He not only knew each of us by name

and face, he knew our wives and girlfriends. He took it personally when we lost people."[1]

Luke and I met for breakfast at the Marriott Hotel the
morning after he arrived. Wynn Tyner, who had come to the
hospital the day Ryan died, was a retired Marriot executive,
and he had arranged rooms for all the SEALs. Luke and I sat
away from the other diners at the restaurant. Luke settled into
his meal, took a sip of coffee, and asked, "What happened?"

I explained to him that I had spoken to Ryan the night
before he died and he was fine. I told him about Amy's early-
morning call, then about the lie that I believed the hospital
told us about Ryan ingesting chewing tobacco. I told him I
checked Ryan and would stake my life on the fact that he did
not aspirate on chewing tobacco. I told him I found Ryan's full
tin of tobacco in his bag and I was 100 percent sure someone
killed him. I said that I had contacted an attorney on Amy's
behalf. Luke listened and analyzed carefully, then answered,
"Good. Keep me posted and let me know if there is anything
you need me to do."

Ryan's untimely death was not the end of his story. God
was not done with Ryan Job. His death was just the beginning
of an amazing story of beautiful coincidences—a story that is
still playing out today, as you will soon see.

THE SEALS

A sixteen-man SEAL platoon is thousands of times more powerful and effective than their number because they function

seamlessly as one fluid organism, simultaneously directing all their aggregate will, violence, and force toward their intended target. The bond they share is hard for outsiders to understand. Many people have never experienced anything like it. SEALs refer to it as "The Brotherhood." Probably the closest relationship to it is the bonds twins share. They sense each other's thoughts and feelings. They can tell from a passing glance when one of their own is upset. They all get the same bad feeling about situations and people at the same moment. They feel each other's pain. The loss of one leaves a deep wound in all.

In a sense, the SEALs exchange their individual DNA for one shared by all who earn the trident, the symbol of the SEALs. The communion between SEALs is welded deep into their souls, transcending all other commitments, including marriage. They are a network of brothers who stand ready to assist, to fight, to kill, and to give their lives for each other. When a SEAL dies, he takes with him a piece of every SEAL who ever served, a portion willingly given by all the members. SEALs are never alone in this world or the next.

COMING FORTH AS GOLD

Ryan's funeral was held on October 1, 2009, at Scottsdale Bible Church. Pastor Jamie presided over the service. There were nearly two hundred Navy SEALs in attendance, both active duty and retired, from all parts of the world. They were in full dress uniform or civilian attire, but they all wore their golden tridents pinned on their uniforms or suit jackets above their hearts. They all sat together on one side of the church, apart from everyone else. Three hundred other friends, family, and mourners filled the pews in the large U-shaped church.

Enlarged photos of Ryan sat on easels on either side of the altar. At the front of the church, the actual weapon Ryan carried when he was wounded was displayed. I was told that his gun is now mounted at a SEAL facility with a plaque under it recounting Ryan's deeds in the alley in Iraq that earned him the Bronze Star. Beside his gun stood his shadow box filled with his medals and awards. A video flashed images of Ryan climbing Mount Rainier, Ryan hunting elk, and other scenes from his life. A song played behind the images:

> *There will be a day with no more tears*
> *No more pain, and no more fears*
> *There will be a day where the burdens of the place*
> *Will be no more, and we'll see Jesus face to face.*[2]

Trey sat in the front pew with Amy. Ryan's SEAL brothers Luke, Tommy, and Chris, Ryan's birth brother, and other pallbearers carried Ryan's flag-draped casket into the church. Luke, Ryan's brother, and I, along with some others, gave eulogies. Other family members and friends spoke. Some of the stories made us laugh; others moved us to tears.

As I mentioned, Ryan and I would often talk about the book of Job and how ironic it was that his name was Job and that he'd been tested as thoroughly as the biblical Job. As Chris put it in reference to the merciless hazing he and others put Ryan through, "We tested him, believe me." When things got tough, I would tell Ryan, "Relax, it's just another test." Then I would quote my favorite Job verse: "But He knows the way that I take; when He has tested me, I shall come forth as gold" (23:10).

A golden trident pin is issued to each Navy SEAL upon graduation from BUD/S. The trident is the most valued possession of every SEAL, worn on every naval uniform above the heart and above all other medals and honors. At the end of Ryan's funeral, his fellow SEALs removed their tridents from their chests, then walked up to Ryan's wooden casket, side by side, each with their trident in hand. Each SEAL placed his most valued possession atop the casket, and with a closed fist and powerful strike, nailed his trident into the wood. Each bang created an echo of frustration, pain, and grief that reverberated through all in attendance.

Nobody spoke. By the time every SEAL had paid his final respects, the casket was covered in gold. Trey and I led Ryan out of the church for the last time while bagpipers played the hymn that old sailor John Newton wrote, "Amazing Grace." As the pallbearers carried Ryan behind us in his golden casket, I turned around and got a final glimpse of my friend, Ryan Job, coming "forth as gold," just like it said in Job 23:10. Just another coincidence, I suppose. Calmness came over me. I felt God again, his sign to me, so unmistakable that it could not be confused with anything else but him. He was close, and I could feel it, just like he said he would be: "The LORD is close to the brokenhearted and saves those who are crushed in spirit" (Ps. 34:18 NIV).

Ryan's remains were cremated.

Chapter Eleven

A HOLLOW VICTORY

★ ★ ★

A SHORT TIME after Ryan's funeral, I was able to connect Amy with Buddy Rake, the lawyer my business attorney had recommended. Buddy was originally from Texas, tall, lean, fit, and soft-spoken, and a Navy veteran. He looked to be in his early fifties, so I was surprised to learn that he was near seventy. Buddy used his Texas charm and easy approach to great effect. His clients had come to know him as an authentic man who cared deeply about finding the truth and delivering justice. Naïve adversaries who mistook him for an unsophisticated good ol' boy fell right into his trap, as he would ruthlessly rip them apart—even before the case went to trial—through a combination of a brilliant legal mind and meticulous preparation. Buddy could thrash his opponents in several different ways. He could out-lawyer them or he could sit back and wait, allowing them to demolish themselves.

I found out later that Buddy was one of the most highly respected attorneys in the state of Arizona, if not the country. Buddy invested in the Phoenix community, where he was a volunteer basketball coach for twenty-five years. In fact, he was one of the winningest coaches in all of Arizona high school sports. He won on the basketball court the same way he won in the courtroom, through meticulous preparation and by outplaying and outcoaching the other team. He was tough, smart, selfless, and fully committed to his mission. If there were a Navy SEAL version of a lawyer, it would have been Buddy Rake.

I urged Amy to meet with Buddy so that she could better understand her legal rights. I had to hand it to her—it was just weeks after Ryan's death, and she was pregnant and studying to take her board certification exam, and I was asking her to explore what could be an explosive and emotional case. Amy called me after her meeting to say she'd hired Buddy to represent her. Buddy wrapped a hedge of protection around her, guarding her with all his skill, knowledge, and experience.

AUTOPSY REPORT

I called Buddy in December and told him I was 100 percent sure that someone had killed Ryan, that every cell in my body told me the hospital was responsible, and that he needed to find the truth. After my passionate rant, he gave me the news that the autopsy report was in. On December 3, 2009, more than two months after Ryan's death, the truth had come out. Ryan had more than five times the amount of Fentanyl that would have been lethal in his system; the amount was shocking to me. I was relieved that the truth was finally out but devastated by the fact that Ryan's death was due to a totally avoidable medical error.

Fentanyl is a narcotic with eighty times the potency of

morphine and fifty times the strength of heroin. In 2004, Fentanyl was responsible for more than 115 deaths in Florida alone.[1] The autopsy report was indisputable. One of the hardest aspects of Ryan's death for me to accept was that it was a Fentanyl overdose, because the effects of Fentanyl (or any opiate drug) can be reversed almost immediately by administering the drug Naloxone. Naloxone is an opioid antagonist that is specifically used to counteract the life-threatening depression of the central nervous and respiratory systems that can occur as a direct result of a drug overdose. If the hospital staff had just done their jobs—what they were paid to do— and made sure that Ryan was connected to his monitors, they would have been instantly alerted to his drop in heart rate and they could have administered Naloxone, which would have saved his life. If I knew that, then Amy knew it too, as she was well versed in this area of medicine.

My emotions were so confused—one minute I was devastated and the next I was irate. I would lie awake at night for months, my mind vacillating between fantasies of revenge and justice. The sleepless nights dragged on until one night I made a peace treaty with myself: in return for the truth, I would let go of the past and forgive the people who killed Ryan.

Ryan's official cause of death was a lethal overdose of pain medication. This, however, did not mean that the case against the hospital was a slam dunk, and Buddy Rake was not one to leave anything to chance. He still needed to file and masterfully manage the lawsuit, which would include countering all the maneuvers put forth by the defense.

THE LAWSUIT

The defendants were many and included all the doctors and medical facilities who provided services to Ryan. Fast-forward to several months after the autopsy report came in. The defendants delivered a dossier of requested documents to the court. One of the documents was a nurse's note that read, "Unexpected death, autopsy pending, that was a result of hospital-acquired injuries." The hospital knew all along that someone on their payroll killed Ryan. During Buddy's meticulous preparation, he found this patient care note. It was as if God had placed the note there for Buddy to discover. Finding this document after seeing the autopsy report stoked Buddy's internal rage, but on the outside he was calm, focused, and carefully working each step of his plan.

The actual complaint was filed in court on June 15, 2010, more than a year after Ryan's death. It was a simple nine-page document outlining the allegations against the defendants. Section fourteen is where the complaint describes Ryan:

> As of September 21, 2009, Ryan Job, age 28, was an Iraq war veteran and a hero who had sustained a gunshot wound to the head while in action in Iraq in 2006. Ryan subsequently underwent numerous successful reconstructive surgeries of his head and face, without complication or untoward results. Apart from the gunshot wound to his head and related blindness, Ryan had no other significant medical history. As of September 21, 2009, Ryan was a Navy SEAL,

war veteran and hero, who was otherwise in top notch physical and medical condition.[2]

It was a brilliantly worded opening salvo. Buddy made sure to include the words *war veteran* and *hero* twice in the four-sentence section. He made sure that everyone knew that Ryan was a Navy SEAL, which implied top-notch physical condition; however, Buddy made sure to spell it out anyway. "Top-notch physical and medical condition" precluded any preexisting conditions that could have led to complications during Ryan's treatment at the hospital.

Section twenty-six of the complaint delivered the knock-out blow that would totally crush the defense:

Ryan Job died on September 24, 2009 as a result of having been negligently and improperly prescribed, recommended, dispensed and administered lethal dosages of and/or lethal combinations of narcotics and respiratory depressants, including but not limited to, Fentanyl, Methadone, Morphine, Ativan, Oxycodone and Benadryl, and as a result of having been negligently monitored after being administered these medications.[3]

These were sobering words, accusations fully supported by the autopsy report. It was also painfully obvious that if the hospital staff had been monitoring Ryan, they would have been alerted to his overdose and could have acted to save him. The physical evidence was irrefutable and most likely enough to sway any jury. However, Buddy was not finished. He would make sure that everyone knew in clear, simple terms that Ryan's untimely death came at the hands of the hospital staff entrusted with his care.

Buddy also wanted to make it unmistakably apparent that Ryan had a full and productive life ahead of him. To prove this, Buddy deposed Ryan's friends and SEAL brothers. Ryan's supervisor at General Dynamics C4 Systems, confirmed that Ryan was employed by the company and had accepted an offer of full-time employment just days prior to his death. This deposition would speak to Ryan's lifetime future earning potential. Luke and Chris gave depositions on Ryan's physical condition, stamina, and recovery since being wounded. Buddy knew that their testimonies and profiles would be provided to the defense, who would have an opportunity to interview both.

Buddy Rake channeled his internal rage into a methodical, step-by-step trap that would force the defense to capitulate before the case ever went to trial. In early December 2011, the case was settled out of court. The *Arizona Republic* newspaper reported the story:

> So, it was a shock when the unlikeliest of events occurred: At 28, Job died because of a mistake at a hospital. . . .
>
> Maricopa County this week agreed to pay $4 million to settle a wrongful-death, medical-malpractice lawsuit that Job's family filed against the county's special health-care district.

Job's death in September 2009 came just two days after successful facial reconstructive surgery at Maricopa Medical Center, run by the Maricopa Integrated Health System.

His family alleged in the lawsuit that he was administered lethal combinations of narcotics and respiratory-depressive medicines after the surgery.

Job's family was never given exact details of what led to the death of the newlywed and father-to-be. In classifying his death, hospital officials placed it in a specific category of preventable errors. That category legally allows hospital officials to keep details of Job's death confidential.[4]

There is no question in my mind that Buddy Rake was 100 percent correct in settling the case. He had his enemy cornered, he gave them his terms of surrender, and they accepted. Buddy was not going to leave anything for a jury to decide. Jury trials are always a toss-up, and Arizona juries are notorious for defying logic. In the hands of a jury, the case could have gone either way, despite the overwhelming evidence in Ryan's favor. We have all seen the shocking conclusions to these types of cases play out on television.

Ryan's death was ruled a "Sentinel Event," which denotes a need for an immediate response, and a "Never Event." *Never Events* are defined as adverse events that are serious and largely preventable. They are the kinds of mistakes that should never happen, such as amputating the wrong limb, doing surgery on the wrong patient, or administering a lethal dose of drugs.

God's hedge of protection was at work again when the nurse's note and other documents were part of the hospital's own records that were sent to the court, revealing that the hospital staff knew full well that they were responsible for Ryan's death the very morning they found him unresponsive in his room. Ryan's death triggered a review of the hospital's official accreditation. Hospitals must have an accreditation in order to stay open. The Maricopa County Medical Center was made to complete a root-cause analysis and create an action plan to correct the mistakes that resulted in Ryan's death. I am confident that these actions helped save lives. Ryan was a great protector, always looking out for others, even in his death.

In the time that it took for the case to settle, Ryan's SEAL teammates had deployed, returned home, and deployed again; some had exited the Navy altogether. Amy graduated from her nurse anesthetist program, passed her board exam, and moved away from Arizona. Ryan's beautiful child was born in April 2010, and as predicted in the Book, it was a girl. "And in all the land were no women found so fair as the daughters of Job" (Job 42:15 KJV). Ryan's daughter has a worldwide network of "uncles" who send her gifts and checks from time to time. She has her daddy's sense of adventure and her mom's great smile.

After details of the settlement had been reported, I called Chris Kyle to let him know that it was over. We talked for a while, and I shared with Chris a few personal conversations Ryan and I had about him and that day on the roof. I let him know that Ryan regretted nothing. Ryan knew that Chris felt guilty for not being the one the sniper shot. I told Chris that the only person Ryan held responsible for his wounds was the enemy that shot him. Chris thanked me for calling. He told me that he had a book coming out and said, "Let's catch up again real soon." The book turned out to be the national bestseller *American Sniper.*

Later that same day I called Luke to tell him that the case was closed and had been settled out of court. Amy and Ryan's daughter was now taken care of. I also shared with Luke that during our long training sessions, Ryan spoke in detail about what a great teacher, leader, and role model Luke was to him. Luke was gracious and humble and pushed the praise on everyone else.

The settlement flexed a wave of emotions in me. It confirmed that my instincts about Ryan's death had been right all along. I was relieved that Ryan's family would have the resources they needed and deserved for the future. I had fulfilled part of the promise I'd made to him that "I will take care of business here." I also felt an overwhelming sense of sadness. I don't know what I was expecting. I had chased the ghost since the day Ryan died, and now years later it had been caught. But in my mind the wrongs have still not been righted. Those who killed Ryan are still working in the health-care industry, being paid well, enjoying their lives, going on vacations, drinking wine with friends, watching their children grow up. They will be there for their children's first days of school, hold them when they are sick, protect them from bullies and dishonest people; they will celebrate birthdays, graduations, and weddings. And yet these people stole all that and more from Ryan.

The settlement was necessary but it was not justice, at least not for me. There was still the moral injury that comes when an institution and its people in places of authority intentionally cover up a grave injustice. The settlement was a necessary, hollow victory. I have forgiven, but I have not forgotten.

Chapter Twelve

ONE WILD, PRECIOUS LIFE

THE POET MARY OLIVER asks: "What is it you plan to do with your one wild and precious life?"[1] Some, like my friend Ryan, give a specific answer: "I will be a pilot, a hunter, a Navy SEAL, a loyal friend, a loving father, and a faithful husband." We all leave a legacy, a footprint on the history of mankind. The length of one's life does not determine one's legacy; rather, it is fashioned by those we influence. Our legacy on this earth is like an endless echo of our lives. It can be heard in the people we have touched. It is our opportunity at immortality, to live beyond the grave. In the short time that Ryan lived after being wounded, he touched all who met him in ways nobody could predict.

★ ★ ★

I have always been fascinated with a field of study in mathematics called chaos theory. The theory states that tiny differences in initial conditions make knowing the long-term future outcome of an event virtually impossible. MIT Professor Edward Lorenz made the concept popular when he termed this "the butterfly effect" in one of his scientific papers entitled "Predictability: Does the Flap of a Butterfly's Wings in

Brazil Set Off a Tornado in Texas?" The professor proved that it could. The flapping wing creates a sensitive change in the initial condition of a weather system, which causes a chain of events leading to unpredictable large-scale phenomena like a tornado.[2] Ryan's life was like the beating of a butterfly's wing, and it caused some magnificent and unpredictable tornadoes.

LUKE'S TORNADO

Who would have thought that Ryan's blindness would have helped his friend Luke find his soul mate? Remember the beautiful table guest at the Navy SEAL gala whom Ryan introduced to Luke? Luke went back to the war, and she continued to report the news. Meanwhile, they e-mailed, talked on the phone, and visited whenever possible. Three years after Ryan introduced them, they married at a ranch in Texas. A sensitive change in his initial condition placed Ryan in the position of matchmaker. If Ryan had not been wounded, he would not have been a guest of honor. If he had not been blind, Luke would not have been there escorting him, thus Luke would have never met his future wife. Years later I met the woman, and she is brilliant, intuitive, thoughtful, and one of the toughest sons of a gun I have ever met. The couple is a perfect match. What a brilliant coincidence.

CAMP PATRIOT

Camp Patriot, the organization that dreamed up therapy programs wrapped in adventures, such as climbing Mount Rainier, became one of Ryan's greatest passions. And in July 2009, he shared it with me. Together Ryan and I traveled to Washington State to join with a new group of wounded veterans who were inspired by Ryan's assault and conquest of Mount Rainier. They would soon take on the mountain themselves. The NFL's Seattle Seahawks football organization was also inspired and pledged its support for Camp Patriot by hosting a pre-climb dinner. Ryan and I arrived along with three other wounded veterans and a small group from Camp Patriot at the Seattle Seahawks stadium to find more than one hundred supporters, all part of a grateful nation who had been inspired by Ryan's triumph on the mountain the year before.

The day after the dinner, Ryan was back at Mount Rainier. This time he carried extra gear up the mountain for the other wounded climbers. The blind Navy SEAL helped lead his wounded brothers up to base camp at 10,100 feet. Ryan left them there, inspired by his effort, and returned down the mountain, allowing each of them to earn back their own dignity on their climb to the summit. None of us suspected that Ryan would be gone forever just two months later. Ryan's story has empowered hundreds of other wounded veterans. He helped set an example of how to live after being wounded.

THE RYAN JOB NAVY SEAL CHALLENGE

In January 2013, the training program that Ryan and I did in his apartment was made into a worldwide online fund-raising event: The Ryan Job Navy SEAL Challenge. Individuals and small groups of supporters from as far away as Connecticut and Australia completed the challenge in Ryan's honor. Camp Patriot coordinated the event, and participants went online and made donations to benefit the organization. Ryan and I loved this training session, and we did our best to "turn each other inside out" by completing each set of exercises as fast as possible and trying to be the first to finish. The fund-raiser was a great opportunity for supporters and Ryan's friends to experience firsthand the challenge and intensity of his training sessions while raising some money for Camp Patriot.

LT. JASON REDMAN, NAVY SEAL

Ryan's passion for Camp Patriot rubbed off on me, and in 2010, I hosted a training camp in Arizona for a group of wounded veterans who would climb Mount Rainier later that summer. Three of the four veterans were Navy SEALs who had been severely wounded in action, one of whom, Lt. Jason Redman, was badly wounded in Iraq. He suffered bullet wounds from a machine gun to his arm and face. He was the guy I mentioned who was in a trench just yards away from his enemy, who was calling to Allah while Jason was imploring God for the strength to live.

In July 2010, the year after Ryan died, Camp Patriot offered me a spot as guide on the Camp Patriot Mount Rainier Summit Challenge Team with the same group of wounded Navy SEALs that I trained with in Arizona. Together, over four days in July we climbed to the summit of Mount Rainier in Ryan's honor. I became friends with Jason, and the two of us kept in close contact. About the same time he also started writing a book and sent me a draft to read. As I sat mesmerized, reading his incredible narrative, I came to the chapter titled "SSITH" about the club that he and two other Navy SEALs had formed. Ryan had told me of the SSITH club (a.k.a. SEALs Shot In The Head) but never mentioned who the other members were. One of the SEALs was Jason, but I never knew it until I read it in the draft of his now-published book, *The Trident*. It was only by coincidence that Jason and I met, climbed a mountain together, and became friends. Ryan had an incredible knack for connecting people. He could even do it from the afterlife. Jason and I remain close friends today.

Chapter Thirteen

CHRIS KYLE

★ ★ ★

WAR IS HUMANITY'S curse upon itself. There are many who would blame God for war, but God has nothing to do with it. Why would God want to destroy his own creation? War is man's doing, and the root cause of war is human free will: one side determined to force their will on the resistant opposition. War isn't just fighting on the front lines. Ryan's friend Chris Kyle was killed far from the battlefield, fighting the war here at home.

I first met Chris in October 2009 at Ryan's funeral, and we kept in contact. He had become a bestselling author, had appeared on television, and had a successful tactical training company with locations in Texas and Arizona. We met up again in mid-January 2012 at the Shot Show, a convention for tactical gear and weapons manufacturers in Las Vegas. We had a few minutes to talk between his book signings and other obligations. People were swarming around us, waiting for a chance to meet him. Chris looked at me and grinned, humbled by it all as he said he was "livin' the dream." He told me that his wife and kids were sick back at home so he didn't mind a few days away, but he missed them. He said he had another book coming out, a story he really wanted to tell and was excited about. He also told me that the only reason he wrote *American Sniper* was that he heard somebody was going to write a story about him, and he wanted to tell his own story his way. The last time we saw each other was at a convention after-party in a Las Vegas nightclub. I told him I would give him a call when things settled down. We said our good-byes and went back to our respective lives.

On a Saturday night three weeks later, Amy's number appeared on my phone. I didn't make it to the phone before it stopped ringing. When I called her back I knew from her voice something was very wrong. My heart raced. She was calm and solemn as she said, "I wanted you to hear it from me before you heard it on TV." She paused. "Chris Kyle is dead."

It was as if the words did not equal their meaning. She continued, "He and a friend were shot and killed a few hours ago at a gun range." I immediately called Luke, who stoically verified the news. Luke would fly to Texas to once again humbly lead the task of coordinating events and taking care of his men and their families.

Chris and his friend Chad Littlefield had offered to help out a veteran who allegedly was having some "readjustment issues." Together the three of them went to a country club with a shooting range, which is not uncommon in Texas. As soon as they arrived, the twenty-five-year-old veteran they were trying to help shot and killed both Chris and Chad.

I never met Chad, but by the description that Chris's wife gave at his funeral, he was a good friend to Chris. They would work out together in the early mornings. They both liked to hunt and were strong Christians and family men. I considered that Chad and I may have been alike in some ways and understood why he and Chris were friends. Like Ryan had confided in me, Chris confided in Chad without fear of judgment. Chad had never been in the military and helped to translate the foreignness of the civilian world to Chris upon his return from war. They respected and watched out for each other. Chad was married with a young daughter, and their lives were now forever changed.

The same wave of anger and sadness flexed inside me as it did that day in the hospital with Ryan. The killer was arrested several hours later driving Chris's truck.

Chris's funeral was held at Dallas Cowboys Stadium. A curious coincidence occurred after I checked into my hotel. The clerk told me that my room payment had been taken care of by the Texas Law Enforcement Association. In fact every room in the hotel was filled with funeral guests, and all charges had been paid by this group. The clerk asked if I would mind sharing a room with another guest rather than having to send guests to other hotels. I said I would be happy to share my room. There were about 250 rooms in the hotel, and people were checking in from all around the world. My roommate could be just about anyone.

As I entered my room and put down my bag, someone else opened the door. It was Tommy, the medic who had rushed up to the roof and worked to save Ryan's life in Iraq. It was an amazing coincidence. He and I caught up on the last four years. He didn't know about the results of Ryan's autopsy or the legal case. Tommy and Ryan had first met in BUD/S, where they were both new guys on the same SEAL team. The two of them became as close as friends and teammates could be. The day that Ryan was shot changed Tommy forever. After escorting Ryan out of the fight to the hospital at Camp Ramadi, Tommy had watched anxiously as doctors at Camp Ramadi took over Ryan's care and went to work to save his life. As we sat talking in the hotel room Tommy told me that it was the intensity of his experience in treating Ryan's wound that made him realize he needed to dedicate his life to medicine. He deployed to Iraq twice more, earning a chest of medals. During that same time he finished his undergraduate degree, applied to medical school, married, and started a family. He was pursuing his medical degree at Harvard Medical School at the time of Chris's funeral. He credited Ryan as his inspiration for pursuing medicine and planned to continue serving in the Navy as a physician and medical researcher. There is no doubt in my mind that Tommy will one day help revolutionize medicine and save countless lives.

Chapter Fourteen

SEARCHING

★ ★ ★

THE PASTOR AT the Bible church was about my age. He wore jeans—no robes or collars. He read a statement I have heard hundreds of times before but never really understood: "Blessed are the poor in spirit, for theirs is the kingdom of heaven" (Matt. 5:3).

"Poor!" the preacher said. "Poor! Do you mean broke? You're still empty, still searching.

"Broke!" he exclaimed. "Or do you mean broken? The losses in your life have left you broken."

Then the preacher said, "Welcome home, friend, God has been waiting for you. He wants a personal relationship with you. He said so right here in this book"—the preacher held up the Bible—"and he's been saying it all along. You just couldn't hear him."

But I did hear him on the hill that day when Ryan and I were hiking. I heard him in the hospital when I asked for help. As the preacher spoke, I felt like he was looking right at me, and it was unsettling. I swore that I could feel people studying him as he stared directly at me.

The preacher paused and leaned forward toward me and said, "No middlemen. He wants to talk directly to you."

I was stunned. It was as if nobody else was in the church. My heart raced and my ears rang. "Is this guy talking to me?" I said under my breath. I half expected him to point at me and say, "Yes, I'm talking to you!" This was the first time in my life that I ever heard the concept of a direct relationship with God.

The preacher continued, "It's all right here in this book." He held up the Bible again. "Reading it is easy. Living it is challenging but well worth it, and when you do ruthlessly live it, then it will take you on the greatest adventure you could ever imagine." I like adventures, and the preacher was right: I was broken and searching. But God sent me a sign one day in the desert that I was on the right track. The sign was a blind guy, leading me to faith.

GOD STALKING

Since that day in church, I have pursued God, or more accurately, I have stalked God. Over the last few years I have encountered him daily and discovered who God has been hanging around with and the scandalous acts that God and his accomplices have been involved in. I found him in the nonprofit organization Camp Patriot. I didn't know it at first, but they are all a bunch of God-fearing Christians. You would never know it from the outside. There's no fish emblem on their old van that picks up disabled veterans, no crosses dangling from any mirrors.

I had my first clue one morning when I was helping to

guide on Mount Rainier. I stopped by one of their hotel rooms before the climb to meet up for breakfast, and on a night table, camouflaged among travel itineraries, drink cups, a phone, and a laptop computer, was a tattered Bible. Later that same morning in the restaurant, they quietly said grace in plain sight of everyone. What makes this group so scandalous is that they've been going around finding wounded veterans, caring for them, and empowering them by offering an amazing adventure that helps to restore dignity, confidence, and hope, and to build new relationships.

The real war is right here at home. According to the government's own statistics, the death toll for veteran suicides at home will soon exceed the number of service members killed in action in both Afghanistan and Iraq. Suicide is a condition of hopelessness, and there is no pharmacological solution for restoring hope. The wound of hopelessness can only be healed through the right relationships.

Now I see God everywhere. I see him in conversations I overhear on airplanes and in coffee shops. On the desert trail that I hiked with Ryan, I found a small sun-bleached pamphlet perched on top of a remote trail marker that outlined the "Good News." I see God in the random people I meet; they all seem to be ambassadors of God in some way. I am no longer stalking God, because he is stalking me. I realize that he has been all along. As I look back over my life, it seems that God has always been there calling to me, encouraging me. Since that day at the Bible church I have stalked God by striving to live my life by the words in the Bible. And as promised, my life has been an amazing adventure ever since. I have climbed high mountains with Navy SEALs and other wounded vets. Some of them have become close friends. I have had the privilege and honor of telling Ryan's story by writing this book, which has been an incredible experience. I continue to work with Camp Patriot in their mission of helping wounded veterans earn back dignity and hope.

I no longer worry about my future career path. One day I took a blind leap of faith and gave up a successful finance career because I wanted to help transform people's lives. Ironically, while I was attempting to transform other people's lives, Ryan transformed my life.

While the world around me swirls with political scandals, family problems, war, abuse of power, divorce, drugs, greed, and fear, I have a loving family. My faith insulates me from that other world. My priorities have changed; my thoughts, language, and beliefs have changed. Faith is a peculiar companion. My faith began as a conversation with doubt, and then through a number of strange coincidences, it became my daily dialogue with God.

EXAMPLES OR WARNINGS

There are those who don't believe in an all-knowing God and rely on science and theory to explain the unknown. There are others who are too afraid to trust in God and rely only on their own abilities and knowledge to navigate life. What if these same people came to the conclusion that they are not in control? What if they simply trusted the fact that nobody really knows how the earth and the universe came about, and that the theory of an all-knowing and all-powerful God is just as valid as any other? What if they gave in to the idea that a divine being made them and wants a direct relationship with them? Would these people have a daily conversation with God? Would they accomplish more, risk more, have less stress, and live like each day was a great gift wrapped in an adventure? Perhaps, but for now their lives act as warnings that expose their untapped potential, fear, and confusion.

Ryan and I made a promise to each other the night before he died: I would take care of business here, and he would take care of business up there. At the time, "up there" meant the upper floor of the hospital where his room was. It means something altogether different now. These were the last words we would ever speak to each other. It's hard to understand how the universe conspired to connect a guy from Boston with a young blind Navy SEAL from Washington in the desert of Arizona, but somehow it happened and we became friends. Ryan kept his promise to me. His ruthless faith overflowed into my life, and this is how he shared the gospel with me. His life was an example of faith and courage, and his death led me to seek a personal relationship with God.

PRIORITIES

A few nights before Ryan died, he told Amy that his priorities were:

1. His Lord and Savior,
2. Her, his wife, and
3. His family and friends.

Job in the Bible had the exact same priorities. He was absolutely certain of his number one too, his Lord and Savior: "For I know that my redeemer liveth" (Job 19:25 KJV). He also knew that his priorities would be tested over and over again, but it was his Lord and Savior, his number one, who gave him the will to face any test.

If you think about it, our priorities shape our entire lives and our futures, for better or worse. Ryan's priority was his faith in his Savior. This is what gave him the courage to face any danger and take on any task. You can't fake your priorities. It's easy to trust God when things are going great, but it's nearly impossible to do when things are not going well or when the wheels completely fall off your life. Ryan's priority was informed by his rational conclusions about faith, that there is no fear or worry when one has faith.

In his short life Ryan Job experienced selfless acts of love and devotion wrapped in the brutality of war. His transformation was not a result of his being wounded. Rather, it was because he accepted Christianity as his next and final adventure. It was a lifestyle that changed his thoughts, which changed his beliefs, which changed his mind and actions.

The great duty of every Christian is to live the faith, all in, full-time, so that when others see you they know that you are different. Most people will never read the Bible, but they will know you and study your life. Your life will be their gospel. True Christians, like Ryan, have a mission—to live like Jesus did. To forgive, to give, to be grateful, to love and inspire by the way you live your life. Ryan was living his mission, working to perfect it each day.

Ryan, like many adult children, had conflicts with his parents, especially his father. These disagreements simmered until the weeks before Ryan died. Apparently he considered the conversation we had about forgiveness and put it into action and mended the relationship with his father. Up until then, the pair had not spoken for some time. Ryan let go of the past and reached out to his father. The two were planning a hunting trip together when Ryan died. Ryan's transformation was absolutely real, and proof was that he applied the healing power of forgiveness. I count this as one of Ryan's greatest accomplishments.

Ryan's last precious gift to me was the inspiration and courage to live my faith, to choose my number-one priority.

EXHAUSTED CAPABILITIES

Ryan passed from this world far too young. He had accomplished so much in such a short time and was truly a noble soul. I am reminded of the eulogy given by Ralph Waldo Emerson of his friend, hero, and inspiration, Henry David Thoreau. Thoreau's sudden death at a young age, like Ryan's, came as a shock to everyone. The last paragraph of his eulogy can only be spoken about a few rare, great people in this world. Ryan Job was one of them.

The country knows not yet, or in the least part, how great a son it has lost. It seems an injury that he should leave in the midst his broken task, which none else can finish,—a kind of indignity to so noble a soul that he should depart out of Nature before yet he has been really shown to his peers for what he is. But he, at least, is content. His soul was made for the noblest society; he had in a short life exhausted the capabilities of this world; wherever there is knowledge, wherever there is virtue, wherever there is beauty, he will find a home.[1]

ANOTHER BLIND GUY

Four years after Ryan's death, I attended a service at Scottsdale Bible Church where Ryan had attended regular Sunday services with Amy and where his funeral was held. Pastor Jamie Rasmussen arrived a few minutes early and was standing at the front. He'd been the one person Amy asked me to call that day years earlier in the hospital when Ryan died. I had not spoken with him since the funeral and decided to reintroduce myself. He said that he remembered me. He told me that he saw the film *Act of Valor* and asked if the scene when the Navy SEAL was shot in the face was about Ryan. I said yes. He inquired about Amy and the baby and asked me to pass along his well wishes.

As the service started, I exited the church to visit the men's room. I had never had allergies before in my life, but for some reason I had a bad case of them with all the classic symptoms: itchy throat, runny nose, etc. I coughed, sneezed, blew my nose, and generally decompressed for a good fifteen minutes before washing up to return to the service. I could hear the music playing. It was then that I experienced a strange and beautiful coincidence. I was alone as I turned to walk down a short hall toward the exit of the men's room when the door punched open and a red-tipped cane with a white shaft poked through the doorway. The next moment a young blind guy and I were facing each other in the narrow men's room hallway with no place for either of us to go. I was stunned; I was now sure that God was stalking me. In the shock of the moment I could feel my eyes well with tears; I would blame it on the allergies.

I said, "Hey, brother, can I point you in the right direction?" He answered with a smile. "Sure, that would be great." He walked toward me, and I placed my hand on his shoulder and pointed him. "The urinals are three feet directly in front of you, the sinks are five feet directly behind, there is one exit and it's the way you came in." He said, "Thanks, got it."

What are the chances of me running into a blind guy alone in a restroom in a place that was first introduced to me by a blind guy? How many blind guys could there be in Scottsdale, Arizona? How many could there be at this church? It didn't matter because like I said, maybe coincidences are how God communicates. I'm not sure what God was trying to tell me. Maybe he just wanted to say hello and see how I liked my new seasonal allergies, which by the way, I've never had again since that day. Allergies so bad that they caused me to visit a men's room that I have never been in before and spend fifteen minutes clearing my head only to turn and face a blind guy who reminded me of my friend Ryan, whom I had just spoken about with the pastor who'd helped lead Ryan to faith and later laid him to rest. Maybe God just wanted to say, "Keep going and don't worry, Bob, I've got you."

I wrote at the start of this book that I believe there are no coincidences in life, no chance meetings and no random events; there is a plan for each of us, a force that brings us together, then twists and binds us into a single length of rope that is attached to our destiny. I said that you were meant to read these words, that this message is for you and is now part of your plan. The message is to have faith, ruthless faith, Job-like faith. A faith so complete it transforms your life from ordinary to extraordinary. A faith that allows you to press on with the certainty that you are never alone in your struggles.

I believe that all of the challenges in our lives are part of God's unique plan for each of us. This plan comes to us over time in parts of a puzzle. Each piece is delivered to us by strangers, friends, family members, and the random people who come into our lives ever so briefly and bring with them a critical piece of the puzzle.

There are some of you who already got this message and are living an amazing faith-filled, adventurous life. There are others who question if there is a plan for them or if there is really an all-knowing God. If you are in this group, then I ask you to consider the idea that the random coincidences in your life might be God's way of communicating with you.

God has been trying to talk to you. He sent so many people, moved so many things around, to get your attention. He even had you read this book. What more evidence do you need? He wants a personal relationship with you. He wants you to pursue him, stalk him if need be, but make him your priority.

This does not mean that you will not experience disappointments, hardships, pain, and suffering, because you will. However, when you place your faith in him, your response to these events will be different from what it was in the past. You will not be a prisoner to despair, apathy, and hopelessness. If you pursue God, learn how he works, and trust that he has a plan for you, then God will speak to you in beautiful, unimaginable coincidences. One day God may even stalk you back.

Our lives are like beams of light. They shine bright through the inspiration and love that we share with others. If you choose to shine your light bright, then it will shine long.

In memory of my friend, a bright light, Ryan Job.

Lessons from Ryan's life:

1. Make God your priority, and everything else will fall into its proper place.
2. Have faith, then let go.
3. Humility will always get you further than pride.
4. Ruthlessly abandon your old ways.
5. Hard work and persistence always earn respect.

6. A great sense of humor is a powerful weapon.

7. No matter how bad life gets, you are never, ever out of the fight.

8. Service to others inspires others to service.

9. Do it now because it's all borrowed time.

10. There is no such thing as a coincidence.

To learn more and see photos of Ryan's story, please visit www.awarriorsfaith.com.

AFTERWORD

SIX YEARS AFTER Ryan's death, his life is still impacting many who knew him.

LT. JASON REDMAN, NAVY SEAL (RETIRED)

Lieutenant Redman is the author of the highly acclaimed book *The Trident*, a memoir of his experience of becoming a Navy SEAL officer and being wounded in action. Jason wrote an inspirational and moving tribute to Ryan in his book. Jason went on to become the founder of Wounded Wear, a nonprofit organization that advocates for wounded and disabled service members.

LUKE

Luke was Ryan's SEAL team commander and was awarded the Bronze Star with Valor for coordinating Ryan's evacuation after he was shot. He cofounded a successful leadership training firm and has been busy transforming organizations across the globe. Ryan introduced Luke to a beautiful television news anchor back in 2008. The couple is now married and has started a family.

TREY

Ryan's loyal guide dog, Trey, was purchased for Ryan by Secretary Donald Rumsfeld through a donation to Southeast Guide Dogs. After Ryan's death, his wife gave Trey to me. A year later, my family moved, and Trey moved to a new home with one of my close friends who also knew Ryan. He is retired now and spends his days opening doors, swimming, lounging, and playing with his two dog companions.

RAMADI, IRAQ

In 2007, the airmen, soldiers, sailors, and Marines of Task Force Bruiser secured the peace in Ramadi. The city and all other areas of Iraq were later successfully turned over to the new Iraqi government. Years later, in 2014, sectarian violence erupted in Ramadi and across the region as Al Qaeda in Iraq morphed into ISIL. Many in the media have erroneously and callously tried to link this instability to a waste of American lives. Former American service members are not responsible for governing or keeping the peace in Iraq. The warriors I know who fought in Ramadi and elsewhere around the globe fought for each other, not for Ramadi, Iraq, Afghanistan, or any other piece of real estate. Risking your life for the people you love is never a waste.

TIMELINE

MARCH 11, 1981: Washington State: Ryan Job is born.

AUGUST 1985: Boston, MA: Robert Vera meets Sean Carter, who would later introduce him to Ryan Job.

1998: Ryan earns his private pilot's license.

OCTOBER 1, 2000: Robert moves to Arizona from Boston.

1999–2002: Ryan attends the University of Washington.

SEPTEMBER 6, 2002: Ryan leaves the University of Washington and enlists in the Navy.

SEPTEMBER 2002: Sean enlists in the Navy.

MAY 2003–NOVEMBER 2004: Ryan's BUD/S experience.

JUNE 2005: Ryan completes Naval Special Warfare Advance Training and is assigned to SEAL Team 3.

JANUARY 2006: Robert leaves his finance career to start an endurance training company.

APRIL 2006: Ryan deploys to Iraq as a member of SEAL Team 3, Task Unit Bruiser, Charlie Platoon.

JULY 2006: Ryan is awarded the Bronze Star for saving his platoon in an alley in Ramadi, Iraq.

AUGUST 2, 2006: Ryan is wounded and made blind on a rooftop in Ramadi, Iraq. Marc Lee is killed.

MARCH 2007: Ryan and Amy are married on the beach in San Diego, California.

AUGUST 2007: Ryan and Amy move to Arizona from San Diego, California.

JUNE 2008: After twenty years without seeing each other, Sean travels to Arizona to meet with Robert.

JUNE 2008: Sean goes to work with Robert and a client asks if Sean knows a Navy SEAL named Ryan Job.

JUNE 2008: Ryan, Sean, and Robert meet for coffee.

JUNE 2008: Robert and Ryan begin training together to climb Mount Rainier.

JULY 2008: Ryan climbs to the summit of Mount Rainier, the highest mountain in his home state.

JULY 2008: Ryan meets Keni Thomas; the pair are part of the team who summit Mount Rainier.

OCTOBER 2008: Ryan and Luke, his former SEAL Team commander, successfully hunt a 980-pound elk.

OCTOBER 2008: Ryan introduces Luke to his future wife at the Navy SEAL Warrior Fund dinner.

JULY 2009: Robert and Ryan travel to Washington State to assist on the climb of Mount Rainier.

AUGUST 2009: Ryan tells Robert that Amy is pregnant.

SEPTEMBER 24, 2009: Ryan dies of a hospital error in Arizona. He was twenty-eight years old.

OCTOBER 2009: Ryan's funeral is held at Scottsdale Bible Church in Arizona.

OCTOBER 2009: Attorney Buddy Rake files a wrongful death suit on behalf of Ryan's widow and unborn child.

APRIL 2010: Ryan's daughter is born.

JULY 2011: Luke is married.

DECEMBER 2011: The hospital pays a settlement in Ryan's wrongful death lawsuit.

JANUARY 2012: Chris Kyle's book, *American Sniper*, is released and dedicated to Ryan and Marc Lee.

AUGUST 2012: Tommy, Ryan's medic, enters medical school.

NOVEMBER 2012: Robert joins with Camp Patriot to help raise funds for a Veterans Ranch Retreat.

FEBRUARY 2, 2013: Chris Kyle and Chad Littlefield are shot and killed assisting a troubled veteran.

FEBRUARY 2013: Robert attends Chris's funeral and meets up with Tommy.

APRIL 2013: Robert encounters a young blind man while attending a service at Scottsdale Bible Church.

JANUARY 2015: The movie *American Sniper* is released.

MARCH 2015: The book *A Warrior's Faith* is released.

ACKNOWLEDGMENTS

I AM GRATEFUL for the many people who offered their support and helped me share this story. You have all been a godsend to me. Special thanks to:

My Lord and Savior, for your faithfulness.

My wife and children, for all your love and support.

Keni Thomas, for your support and willingness to share your wisdom in the foreword of this book.

Carmen Berry, for seeing the value in my story and pushing me ahead with your words of encouragement.

Chip MacGregor, president of MacGregor Literary. I could not ask for a better agent. Thank you for believing in my story and for showing me how to become a writer.

Kristen Parrish, editor in chief at Thomas Nelson/HarperCollins. Thank you for living this story with me and for your editing skills, which crafted my words into this book.

Aaron, my other brother, for your love and support.

Mike Day, for living like the miracle that you are! I am grateful for your friendship.

The Job family, I love you all.

Sean Carter, my friend from Boston, for his service to this nation and for introducing me to Ryan.

Jason Redman, you inspire me; thank you for your friendship and support.

Scott McEwen, for your friendship and support of this book.

Joe Anderson, for your faith in me.

Megan Keller, for your passion, drive, love, and support over the years.

Nanette Walkley, thank you for coming into my life and for your support.

Dr. John Homer, and to all the men and woman of Charlie Medical, for volunteering for the assignment in Ramadi, for caring for Ryan, and for sharing your experience with me.

Dr. Darryl DelHousaye, president of Phoenix Seminary. Thank you for sharing with me your love of the obscure Old Testament book of Job.

Jamie Rasmussen, senior pastor of Scottsdale Bible Church, where I sit each Sunday and take copious notes as you successfully defend the Christ-centered life. Thank you for making the Bible relevant in my life.

Buddy Rake, Esq. Thank you for taking care of Ryan's family and for your friendship.

Rowin Floth. I am forever grateful for your friendship

and support. Thank you for seeing the value of my story and encouraging me to share it.

Micah and Bill Clark of Camp Patriot, for all that you have done for our veterans. Your friendship continues to be one of the greatest blessings in my life.

Crystal Strimple, for caring for Trey and for being a great friend to Ryan and me.

Wynn Tyner, for your friendship and tireless support of our veterans.

Mike Flood and the NFL Seattle Seahawks organization, for your support of Camp Patriot and all the other veteran organizations that you lift up, and for being such a great friend to Ryan.

Mike and Ruth Casey, for your friendship and love.

The Lester family, for your amazing, beautiful faith.

Bob Cursio and all the great people at General Dynamics C4 Systems in Scottsdale, Arizona, for recognizing Ryan's many talents and bringing him onto the team.

Dr. Steve Blank, for your friendship and support.

To the members of SEAL Team 3, Charlie Platoon. Thank you for your support of this book.

And lastly, to all the great patriots who have worn the uniform and sacrificed for this nation, thank you for your service and for my freedom. You are all in my prayers.

NOTES

CHAPTER 1

1. On August 3, 1857, Frederick Douglass delivered a "West India Emancipation" speech at Canandaigua, New York, on the twenty-third anniversary of the event. www.lib.rochester.edu/index.cfm?PAGE=4398.

2. Chris Kyle with Scott McEwen and Jim DeFelice, *American Sniper: The Autobiography of the Most Lethal Sniper in U.S. Military History* (New York: HarperCollins, 2012), dedication.

3. Ibid., 213–14.

CHAPTER 2

1. Gregg Zoroya, "If Ramadi Falls, 'Province Goes to Hell,'" USATODAY.com, July 11, 2004, http://usatoday30.usatoday.com/news/world/iraq/2004-07-11-ramadi-usat_x.htm.

2. Thomas E. Ricks, *The Gamble: General Petraeus and the American Military Adventure in Iraq, 2006–2008* (New York: Penguin, 2010), 330.

3. Chris Kyle with Scott McEwen and Jim DeFelice, *American Sniper: The Autobiography of the Most Lethal Sniper in U.S. Military History* (New York: HarperCollins, 2012), 227.

CHAPTER 3

1. Eugene. Park, Joshua D. Bell, and Andrew J. Baker, "Traumatic Brain Injury: Can the Consequences Be Stopped?," *Canadian Medical Association Journal* 178, no. 9 (2008): 1163–70, http://www.ncbi.nlm.nih.gov/pmc/articles/PMC2292762/.

2. "What Is the Glasgow Coma Scale?," brainline.org, http://www.brainline.org/content/2010/10/what-is-the-glasgow-coma-scale.html.

CHAPTER 5

1. Graham Collier, "On Meeting Carl Gustav Jung," *The Conscious Question* (blog), *Psychology Today*, February 8, 2012, http://www.psychologytoday.com/blog/the-consciousness-question/201202/meeting-carl-gustav-jung.

2. "Avalanche Heroine Praised for Saving Lives of Climbers," LATimes.com, June 14, 1998, http://articles.latimes.com/1998/jun/14/news/mn-59740.

3. Jack Brown, "Trio of Injured Iraq Veterans Stands Tall on Rainier," SeattleTimes.com, July 11, 2008, http://

seattletimes.com/html/localnews/2008045927
_rainier11m0.html.

CHAPTER 6

1. Andrew B. Newberg, MD, and Mark Robert Waldman, *How God Changes Your Brain* (New York: Ballantine Books, 2009), 51–52.

2. Ibid., 54.

3. Ibid., 53–55.

4. Ibid., 55.

5. William E. Phipps, *Amazing Grace in John Newton: Slave Ship Captain, Hymn Writer, and Abolitionist* (Macon, GA: Mercer University Press, 2001), 205.

CHAPTER 7

1. Chris Kyle with Scott McEwen and Jim DeFelice, *American Sniper: The Autobiography of the Most Lethal Sniper in U.S. Military History* (New York: HarperCollins, 2012), 218.

2. Nicholas Schmidle, "In the Crosshairs," *New Yorker*, June 3, 2013, http://www.newyorker.com/magazine/2013/06/03/in-the-crosshairs.

CHAPTER 8

1. Craft International, "History of the Craft Skull," accessed September 19, 2014, http://www.thecraft.com/craft_skull.html.

2. Ibid.

CHAPTER 10

1. Chris Kyle with Scott McEwen and Jim DeFelice, *American Sniper: The Autobiography of the Most Lethal Sniper in U.S. Military History* (New York: HarperCollins, 2012).

2. Jeremy Camp, "There Will Be a Day," *Speaking Louder Than Before*, BEC Recordings, November 25, 2008.

CHAPTER 11

1. Evelyn Pringle, "Fentanyl Deaths—Severe Math Problems of FDA," LawyersandSettlements.com, March 27, 2006.

2. Kelly Job v. Maricopa County, et al., No. CV2010 −016758, section XIV, http://archive.azcentral.com /ic/pdf/ryan-job-family-lawsuit.pdf.

3. Ibid., section XXII.

4. Michelle Ye Hee Lee, "Navy SEAL Ryan Job: A Portrait of Determination, Tragedy," *Arizona Republic*, December 3, 2011, http://www.azcentral.com/news /articles/2011/11/30/20111130navy-seal-ryan-job -portrait-determination-tragedy.html.

CHAPTER 12

1. Mary Oliver, "The Summer Day," *New and Selected Poems*, (Boston: Beacon Press, 1992), 94.

2. Edward Lorenz, *The Essence of Chaos* (Seattle: University of Washington Press, 1993), 181–84.

CHAPTER 14

1. Ralph Waldo Emerson, *The Conduct of Life, Nature, and Other Essays* (London: J.M. Dent & Sons and New York: E.P. Dutton, 1908), 74.

ABOUT THE AUTHOR

ROBERT VERA began his professional career in politics as a staff assistant to a US senator, where he managed military and veteran affairs. Upon leaving government, Robert enjoyed a twenty-year career in the finance industry. In 2006, after feeling a need to become more significant in people's lives, he took a leap of faith to follow his dream to become an entrepreneur. Robert serves on a number of nonprofit boards and as a mentor to returning veterans. He earned his bachelor's degree in political science from Boston College. He is married with two children and lives in Phoenix, Arizona.